T5-BAZ-852

Paraverbal Communication with Children

Not through Words Alone

Paraverbal Communication with Children

Not through Words Alone

Evelyn Phillips Heimlich
and
Arlene J. Mark

Foreword by
Harlow Donald Dunton

PLENUM PRESS • NEW YORK AND LONDON

ISBN 0-306-43624-8

To protect the privacy of individual patients, names, places,
and other identifying facts contained herein have been fictionalized.

© 1990 Plenum Press, New York
A Division of Plenum Publishing Corporation
233 Spring Street, New York, N.Y. 10013

Printed in the United States of America

Foreword

For over twenty years I have been privileged to observe, participate in, and contribute to the development of the ideas and
techniques that culminated in this most unusual, impressive,
and useful book.

While it is difficult to convey in words the total experience
of this innovative therapeutic approach, this volume enables
the reader to become a part of these therapy sessions and to
learn to "know" and appreciate these fruitful methods.

The techniques described in detail in this volume are
designed for use with children who are viewed as "resistant" and uncommunicative—a fairly large percentage of
youth who have not responded to traditional therapy. The
approach is based on many practical assumptions. Among
them are the idea that rhythm, of whatever nature, cannot
be "shut out"; that one can have pleasure in producing com-

munication (fun of all things); and that pleasure and acceptance lead to the integration of motility, emotions, and ideation. These all lead to increased self-esteem and competence. The selection of the modality is completely individualized and leads to a therapy *with* the child—not *to* or *at* the child.

To complete the circle, the method is eminently teachable. Thus, both students in training and practicing therapists who are concerned with promoting growth and development in the children they treat will find this guide exceptionally useful and stimulating.

H. D. Dunton, M.D.

Clinical Professor of Psychiatry
Columbia University College of
Physicians and Surgeons
New York, New York

Acknowledgments

The author would like to take this opportunity to acknowledge our debt of gratitude to the many people who participated in the development of Paraverbal Communication as presented in this book. Our greatest feeling of gratitude goes first of all to all those children whose communication needs stimulated both of us to find ways of helping them. Deep appreciation goes also to Dr. Sydney G. Margolin, who gave the name Paraverbal Therapy to the method after reviewing some of the children's problems and Mrs. Heimlich's work with them. Profound thanks also go to Dr. Harlow Donald Dunton, as both Mrs. Heimlich's supervisor and mentor in the Child Psychiatry Department at the New York State Psychiatric Institute, where he served as head of the Department of Child Psychiatry. Gratitude goes as well to Dr. Anne Hardesty, who for years analyzed weekly the

Paraverbal Communication Method work being done with inaccessible children. Thanks also to Dr. Daniel Stern, who repeatedly analyzed videotapes of Paraverbal Communication sessions and who designated the sound and movement techniques used in Paraverbal Communication as maneuvers. The help of Evelyn Heimlich's brother Robert Phillips was invaluable in reviewing the presentation style of the material in the book. To Evelyn's son, Arthur, go thanks for patient review of the material and for supplemental typing. Our thanks go as well to Bernard Mazel, who recognized the unique contribution of the Paraverbal Communication Method.

And finally, profound appreciation goes to our husbands, Milton Heimlich and Reuben Mark, without whose cheerful and generous support this book would never have come to be realized.

We gratefully acknowledge permission to reprint lyrics for the following songs from the sources indicated:

"Russians" by Sting. ©1985 Magnetic Publishing Ltd./Reggatta Music, Ltd. Used by permission. All rights reserved.

"Be Good Johnny," words and music by Colin Hay and Greg Ham. ©1982, 1983 April Music Pty. Limited. All rights for the USA and Canada controlled and administered by Blackwood Music Inc. All rights reserved. International copyright secured. Used by permission.

"Pressure," by Billy Joel. ©1981, 1982 Joel Songs. All rights controlled and administered by EMI Blackwood Music Inc. All rights reserved. International copyright secured. Used by permission.

"Growing Up," words and music by Lawrence Smith and Jalil Hutchins. ©1986 Zomba Enterprises Inc./Funk Groove Music Inc. (administered by Zomba Enterprises Inc.)/Zomba Music Publishers Ltd. All rights controlled by Zomba Enterprises Inc. for USA and Canada. All rights reserved. Used with permission.

"Comfortably Numb" by David Gilmour/Roger Waters. ©1979 Pink Floyd Music Publishers Inc. Used with permission.

"Another Brick in the Wall" by Roger Waters. ©1979 Pink Floyd Music Publishers Inc. Used with permission.

E.P.H.
A.M.

Contents

xi

Introduction

Unreachable children are a serious concern to the therapists and teachers who care for them. These professionals often become frustrated because they are unable to gain and maintain the interest of an increasing number of inaccessible children. Paraverbal Communication has been used and researched for the past 20 years and has enabled these professionals to assist many children to overcome emotional and cognitive difficulties.

Paraverbal Communication provides the professional with a unique alternate method to help children achieve their potential. The basic difference between Paraverbal and other therapies for children and adolescents is that the Paraverbal Method emphasizes communication by a reciprocal exchange of feelings and thoughts, which can actually change the behavior of the children involved. Reciprocity

3

between the professional and child is emphasized in Paraverbal Communication with continued shared pleasure being an essential part of Paraverbal sessions. This shared pleasure helps form a trusting relationship and increases the likelihood of eventual communication on a higher level. Although all therapies share the goal of developing appropriate behavior, many do not employ the necessary variety of materials nor the accompanying flexibility for the use of these materials that some inaccessible children require.

The Paraverbal Method is effective with children of all ages. Paraverbal maneuvers offer children the means to discharge tension, ventilate feelings, and develop their emotional and cognitive potential. Young children and adolescents can choose appealing materials through which they can engage in active maneuvers that stimulate and involve them at their individual developmental levels and interests. The child is free to choose and use materials in any constructive way, inspired by his or her needs of the moment. The child is able to maintain appropriate behavior and impulse control because of the structure inherent in the Paraverbal maneuvers, which will be fully illustrated in the book through clinical examples. This opportunity for the child to communicate needs and feelings in his or her chosen, pleasurable way and to feel accepted by the professional is basic to the establishment of needed trust in therapy and is the rationale of the Paraverbal Method. These important emotional components of self-esteem—pleasure, ongoing acceptance, and trust—contribute to the improvement of the child and increase the possibilities for the child's potential in both behavioral and cognitive areas.

Paraverbal Communication, although possessing unique and innovative elements, is grounded in the theories of such child specialists as Daniel Stern, Margaret Mahler, Erik Erikson, Jean Piaget, and others, who have each helped explain human development from infancy to adulthood. In this book, their theories are shown to be the basis of specific

Paraverbal maneuvers. Professionals can employ the Paraverbal Method as a primary therapy or in conjunction with other therapies because the method is solidly grounded in accepted principles of child development.

Throughout this book, the *therapist* refers to any professional involved in helping children, including teachers, social workers, psychologists, and all mental health workers. Using the Paraverbal Communication method, each of these therapists communicates with the child according to that child's immediate needs and sensorimotor preferences.

The materials employed in the maneuvers may include finger paints, elastic ropes, hoops, soap bubbles, water, clay, a variety of simple percussion and string instruments, song lyrics, and other evocative visual and tactile elements. These materials are often used metaphorically to enable children to ventilate feelings acceptably. A child can choose large cymbals and strike them together to dramatize angry feelings more comfortably than just verbally stating that anger. It is less threatening for the child to address these angry feelings, because feelings are first ventilated through the materials, than if directly confronted. Through this process, the child feels safe communicating about the issues contributing to his or her difficulties. Adolescents respond to the metaphoric use of rock music lyrics to readily explain their own wishes and fears and to communicate feelings about their roles in society. The maneuvers do not replace verbal communication but are used *alongside* it to enhance its effectiveness and enable children to experience competence and mastery. Materials are chosen for use in each session according to the referral problem and the therapist's understanding of the child. Although some of the materials used in the method are similar to those found in play therapy or traditional verbal therapy, the materials used in the Paraverbal Method are used for their specific communicative function. They focus on:

1. Opening the lines of communication between the therapist and child

2. Empowering the child by permitting the child to choose materials that help communicate the child's needs and issues

3. The therapist's understanding of the therapeutic use of specific materials, when to use them, and the length of time to continue using them, indicated by cues observed from the child's own responses

Therefore, with Paraverbal maneuvers, therapists can add to their current effectiveness in assisting children by offering them a therapeutically rich choice of materials to help them communicate and function more effectively.

All materials are easy to use for children and therapists alike. In an initial session, an anxious child experiencing low self-esteem may choose and tap a simple drum or clash together a pair of cymbals without making a mistake. As a result, repeated success with such simple rhythmic percussive maneuvers stimulates the child to make other choices with which the child also experiences success and from which the child gains pleasure. Gradually these repeated, pleasurable experiences increase the child's self-confidence and contribute to feelings of competence and mastery, core factors necessary for achieving improved communication and behavior. Children enjoy communicating through Paraverbal maneuvers. They are eager to make choices, ventilate, experience mastery, and in the process, communicate.

I

The Paraverbal
Communication Method

1

Why Children Do Not Communicate and Who Is Referred for Therapy

Why children do not communicate is a complex problem that still needs a great deal of research. One cause is the overall and pervading problem of anxiety. In children, anxiety must be dealt with promptly and consistently. The roots of anxiety can be emotional or organic.

Anxious children who do not communicate require a mostly nonverbal social interactive approach, so that satisfactory communication can develop. For this development to occur, therapy needs to take place in an atmosphere of ongoing acceptance and pleasure. Unless this concept is borne in mind and practiced by the therapist, progress cannot take place, as the anxiety prevents children from dealing with their problems. For example, if a child cannot master age-appropriate language, the child develops a low self-esteem and a concomitant feeling of anxiety. Another example is in the behavioral area, where a child is so withdrawn that the child is unable to participate in games, whether in the playground or in therapy. It should be understood that the problems are indeed part of and contribute to this very anxiety. When such children are consistently helped in Paraverbal Communication, they are able to achieve their potential.

Inappropriate and Disproportionate Reactions

An additional factor that adds to the inability of some children to communicate is that they often react inappropriately and disproportionately to what is said to them. For example, if such a child is asked a direct question, given a comment, or even given simple directions, for a game or for making a drawing, the child feels threatened, and the anxiety level can become so high that communication becomes impossible. Sometimes, too, the lack of skill in verbal communication robs a child of a good self-image, among other things. Such deficits compound the child's inability to communicate. What needs to be pointed out here is that many of these noncommunicating children are often of average or above average intelligence. For various reasons, there are roadblocks that prevent them from communicating. Brief illustrative examples of these children are given at the end of this chapter. In addition, there are whole chapters in the book that are devoted to other individual unusually unresponsive children.

Behavior Disorders

Some of these children have behavior disorders such as muteness, articulation problems, withdrawal, or aggressiveness. For communication with them to take place, as with everyone, they need to understand and be understood. They too, need an approach that provides a purposeful and consistent method that will obviate the disorganizing effects aroused in them by conventional approaches.

Examples of Children Referred for Therapy

The following are examples of children who have been referred for therapy. These children were referred by various sources, including schools, private therapy practices, in- or out-patient clinics, and hospitals. All communicated poorly and were unresponsive to traditional therapies.

These descriptions illustrate possible areas where Paraverbal Communication is found to be helpful with children who do not communicate. All of the children described below were either average or above average in intelligence.

A.R., a nine-year-old adopted girl, presented as hyperactive, hostile, nomadic, and aggressive with little children. She had an insatiable desire for gifts, which resulted in theft behavior. She also exhibited attention deficit, difficulty in school, excessive sensitivity to sound, and passive-aggressive personality trait disturbances. Although verbal, she would not participate in verbal or play therapy. She responded well in the hospital after Paraverbal Communication and was discharged home after 2 years with a recommendation for family therapy.

P.A. is a five-year old boy of high intelligence; he is the youngest of three children with a brother age 15 and a sister age 13. He was withdrawn and preoccupied with death. Socializing was inadequate and he had stopped eating and talking at the time of hospitalization. He did not respond to traditional therapy, standing in a corner with his back to the therapist; however, he did respond to Paraverbal Communication—at first only to non-

verbal aspects, then to song lyrics, and ultimately
to verbal communication as well. He was discharged to a residence, where he became well integrated into the school milieu.

   E.T., a six-year-old elective mute girl, would
talk only to her parents and two brothers, age 10
and 3. She felt unloved. On examination, it was
felt that there was no evidence of organic dysfunction regarding her lack of speech. The therapist
thought the speech disturbance might be related
to some sexual preoccupation. The child was described as rigid and brittle. The therapist felt that
the mutism caused the parents a great deal of
anxiety that was projected onto the mute child
and was her way of manipulating the environment. Her parents reported she was fearful about
talking to people outside the family. School staff
said she joined classmates in singing but not in
talking. At age 3, she was given a clean bill of
health at the nursery, but never spoke even at that
early age, according to the family report. They
also reported that currently she ran out of the
bedroom at night, where she slept with her two
brothers. After three years of Paraverbal Communication, her communication improved and she
was discharged. She said she did not speak because she feared she would be misunderstood,
make mistakes, and be scolded.

   The next three children were adolescents from minority
groups. They were seen as a group and sent to Paraverbal
Communication sessions because they could not or would
not communicate. All were in difficulty with the authorities.
All were inaccessible to traditional therapy and to classroom
learning. All were high school boys who were discharged
from a residence so that they could return to living at home
and attend their high school in the Bronx.

G.T., a 16-year-old black boy, comes from a large family. The mother is a prostitute and one brother is in a residential home because of disciplinary problems. He is undersized and dominated by his brothers, as well as his classmates. He is suspicious, manipulative, has severe feelings of inferiority, is easily frustrated, shy, frequently sarcastic, and disruptive. He could do well in mathematics, if his interest could be elicited. He has difficulty in the language arts and is interested in sports.

M.T., a 16 year-old Puerto Rican ninth-grade boy, lives with his mother and three siblings. The family is on welfare, and the father's whereabouts are unknown. He is regarded by his mother as the man of the house. He likes athletics, truants from school, has difficulty in the language arts, both speaking and reading. (His mother is depressed and never replies to requests for her to come to school.) M.T. is suspicious, often surly, and, although he presents a cocky attitude, cannot be engaged in anything that appears to be new and challenging in the classroom. Efforts at simplifying age-appropriate cognitive materials bring scorn and anger.

J.R. is a 16-year-old, ninth-grade black boy, one of two siblings. The family is on welfare, the father's whereabouts unknown. His mother works sporadically. The boy is very anxious, lies to impress strangers, is exhibitionistic, restless, sarcastic, challenging to authority, disruptive, suspicious, and a truant.

Paraverbal Communication was a source of pleasure and satisfaction to each of these boys who were eager to return week after week. In total, they were involved in Paraverbal Communication for one term. During this time, they were able to make both social and cognitive progress.

2

Paraverbal Communication and Why It Works

Paraverbal Communication is a multisensory, interactive method developed to help therapists who work with unresponsive children unable to be reached by traditional means. Briefly, the term *paraverbal* means parallel with verbal. This means that speech is frequently substituted for by a rich sensorimotor armamentarium of therapeutic materials for interactive communication by the therapist and child. These interactions are known as *maneuvers* and are used according to the child's moment-to-moment needs and behavior as observed by the therapist. In other words, basic to Paraverbal Communication is the idea that speech and dialogue, when used in the treatment of the resistant child, are themselves often threatening and inhibit communication.

The rationale underlying Paraverbal Communication is that, if the child can be engaged through means, frequently

nonverbal, that are pleasurable, the child can be made to feel
accepted and to trust. Then the needed therapeutic relationship can be established. At this point, the child will be able
to discharge tension, as well as ventilate ideas and feelings,
both nonverbal and verbal.

The Paraverbal method is one of observation, assessment,
and treatment. While observing and assessing a child's behavior through an interactive sensorimotor maneuver, the
therapist can choose any of a variety of appropriate maneuvers to address the specific, observed needs of the child (see
Chapter 3). From its communicative structure, the Paraverbal Communication method is unique in its observational
setting for eliciting communication behavior. That is, the
many ways the child uses the materials he selects for his
unique use provide the therapist an opportunity to observe
body movement, facial expression, and other indicators of
development. For example, a child who hesitates to use finger paint or uses it inappropriately can alert the therapist to
possible atypical manifestations. If a child uses Play-Doh for
throwing or cutting instead of the typical use of the material
for squeezing or folding, it can alert the therapist to possible
hidden anger, anxiety, or other behavior not manifested on
the surface.

Paraverbal Communication, with its engaging sensorimotor approach, reduces the often disorganizing effects
aroused in the child by standard therapies. Innovative pleasureful sensorimotor strategies focus on communication as a
bridge to social and cognitive development. Paraverbal Communication techniques are used for children ranging in age
from early childhood through adolescence.

The interactive behavior on the part of the therapist and
the child is of the essence in the Paraverbal Communication
method. This interactive behavior is fundamental to the establishment of communication between the child and the
therapist. Its consistent use forms one of the major differences between Paraverbal Communication and other ap-

proaches, because the primary task of the Paraverbal child–therapist dyad is communication. The interactive exchange of feelings and thoughts that ensue from this pleasureful, spontaneous, mostly nonverbal method helps to change the behavior of those involved. An example of this child–therapist interaction can be seen in the use of a simple sound maneuver; the child begins a session with a short tapping pattern usually spontaneously made up after picking up a drum or other percussion instrument. The therapist observes and immediately interacts and reciprocates by copying the pattern. Then, the therapist taps the rhythm either louder or softer to give variety to the interchange and thus helps maintain attention. After this, the rhythm is repeated, but this time the therapist may vary the pattern by tapping it slower or faster. This additional variation affects the child according to the child's current behavior whether restless or withdrawn. At times, the child may respond to the softness and slowness by becoming quieter if the child happens to be restless or hyperactive at the moment of the tapping. On the other hand, if the child is withdrawn at that moment, the child may be stimulated to be more active and more involved on hearing the louder and faster sounds. All this observed behavior is a form of nonverbal communication to the therapist who then responds in kind, but more intensely, and nonverbally, to what the child has just revealed by responding to the dynamics of loud and soft and/or fast and slow sensorimotor communication.

The maneuvers and ways that are used in Paraverbal sessions put the child in a social situation where there is immediate mutual exchange of communication between the child and the therapist. Interactive maneuvers can be used both reciprocally or synchronously, with child or therapist each participating as the needs of the moment demand. In this way, among other things, shared simultaneous interacting is achieved. Repeated success with the various simple sound or movement maneuvers used in Paraverbal Commu-

nication gradually raises the child's self-esteem and gives
him a feeling of competence and mastery, core factors necessary in helping to achieve improved communication and resultant appropriate behavior. Since the materials require
little or no skill and can be used in any unique way the child
and the therapist desire in their interactive behavior, they are
free to interact spontaneously in this therapeutic social
situation.

A valuable communicative aspect of the sensorimotor
materials used in the maneuvers is the tactile experience
they provide for the child when he becomes involved with
them. In the course of this involvement, affect develops, often followed by the child's spontaneous descriptive words,
leading to the desired communication. The tactile element is
of importance in communication to help engage the child
and elicit affect. To paraphrase Frank in his definitive work
on nonverbal communication, interpersonal relations without tactile communication would be bare and largely meaningless with a minimum of affective coloring or emotional
provocation.

An example of affect stimulated by the tactile experience follows: a child may choose a tactile material such as a
lump of colored clay and feel stimulated to use it metaphorically in a movement maneuver. The child might pound
the clay violently and squeeze it. During this rousing tactile
experience, the child can thus achieve release from anxiety
and possible hidden anger. As a result, one of the children
felt free to verbalize about his hidden home problem and
spontaneously commented while pounding the clay, "That's
what you'll get if you take your brother's toys and don't listen to me." Such an eruption of spontaneous affective verbalization during the continuous metaphoric manipulation
of the clay often forms a bridge to further communication.
This increasing freedom and willingness to communicate
can then develop into the desired, more appropriate
behavior.

A different example of the use of the tactile aspect of the Paraverbal maneuver can be found in the way still another child used a drum of his choice in a sound-dominated maneuver. This child was an angry, anxious 8-year-old boy. He was too anxious to verbalize feelings and thoughts. However, he was able to spontaneously bang on the drum he selected, experiencing, among other things, the tactile benefit, as well as the resultant affect from his movements. The child's motions and how long he chose to discharge anger in this way were closely observed by the therapist. They were signals and signs for the beginning steps toward communication. Before the drum-pounding experience, the child was too anxious to verbalize his feelings and thoughts about severe punishment at home, which was swift and violent. When the therapist interacted with him and joined in his vigorous pounding movement and touching of the clay, he was reassured as the therapist made equally intense accompanying movements on her drum. In this way, there could more readily be ventilation of feeling, channeled through the reciprocal or synchronous movement, which gave the child the needed feeling of acceptance that was so sorely missing at home. The boy felt approved of and his positive self-esteem could begin to emerge. Trust, too, could develop with this first simple step. The door to communication was open. Only then could hidden anger and its attendant anxiety be safely communicated and revealed. His experience was reinforced through the pleasure and satisfaction gained from the freedom of movement that came from the loudness of his pounding the drum. This experience also helped this needy child to feel nurtured. In addition, the mirrored intensity of the facial and bodily expression of the interacting therapist contributed still further to the child's ability to communicate. During the course of this therapeutic remedial work, it should be borne in mind that the therapist is actually only simulating emotions and therefore remaining objective in order to support the child in the sensorimotor communication.

In addition to having the tactile experience through the touching of instruments and other materials, a child and therapist can achieve the needed intimacy through the appropriate reciprocal touch of both the child and therapist, structured by a movement maneuver. For example, child and therapist can hold large metal cymbals in both hands and tap together while chanting, "We tap softly, we tap softly" then, "We tap loud, we tap loud." A number of other variations can then be incorporated into the maneuver such as the use of smaller cymbals with a repetition of the tapping. A further expansion of the movement interaction is the synchronous rhythmic clapping together of the child and the therapist's hands with an accompanying chant: "We clap our hands together, now we clap softly." Variations of loud, fast, slow, and other ways of clapping can be added for further tactile stimulation and interaction. In all of the above ways, the tactile element, so integral a part of the Paraverbal Communication method, helps provide the needed affect for meaningful communication.

Motor experience is another highly significant aspect of Paraverbal Communication and can take place in a variety of situations, such as the child and the therapist reciprocally tapping bongo drums or each other's instruments. Motor experience can also occur as the child and the therapist catch balls, smash soap bubbles, or engage in dramatization. These movement maneuvers permit both motor and tactile experiences to help the child communicate. Mittleman (1954) has called particular attention to the therapeutic significance of motility, describing it as "one of the most important avenues for exercising such functions as mastery, integration, reality testing and control of impulses."

Structure and control of the sessions are implemented through the use of the therapist's own facial expression and body movement, as well as her prosodic changes. This refers to changes in accent, tempo, and volume of the responses, as well as silence. It is important to understand the significance of prosody in the context of establishing communication, because phrases take on different meanings depending on the emphasis of particular words. For example, one can simply state, "I like you." However, by emphasizing the word *I*, the sentence "*I* like you" takes on a slightly different meaning. By emphasizing the word *like*, a still different meaning is achieved by "I *like* you." Finally, with the emphasis on the word *you*, another meaning is communicated by "I like *you*."

A further constructive facet of this prosodic communication technique can serve both as stimulus and possible model for the child to imitate as the child learns to vary the accent, tempo, and volume appropriate to the situation. Therefore, the child learns how to communicate different ideas by varying and controlling his or her own responses. This new communicative facility adds to a child's sense of mastery and therefore development.

In Paraverbal Communication, materials are frequently used metaphorically to enable children to ventilate feelings acceptably and without anxiety. By metaphorically is meant that the materials are used in the way a figure of speech is used; that is, to illuminate one dimension of an object by drawing attention to its similarity to another. An example is "A Mighty Fortress Is Our God." In similar fashion, through Paraverbal Communication, an abused child, working with finger paint, might be heard to say while rhythmically moving his or her hand through the paint, "It's like blood," or "It's blood." At this point, the sensitive, informed therapist can make an appropriate response related to the reported violence in the child's life and thus stimulate further communication, therapeutic to the child. The materials employed metaphorically may include finger paints, elastic ropes, soap bubbles, water, clay, a variety of simple percussion and string instruments, and song lyrics as well as other evocative visual and tactile materials.

Because feelings are first ventilated through the materials used in the maneuvers rather than the child being confronted verbally and directly, it becomes less threatening for the child to address often hidden feelings. Through this safe, metaphoric process, the child feels secure in communicating about the issues contributing to his or her difficulties. The technique serves the significant purpose of liberating the child to use the metaphoric materials as a bridge to further communication and development.

A unique therapeutic value of the Paraverbal use of metaphor is its flexibility. Not only are materials used metaphorically, but song lyrics may be used as well. Song lyrics used metaphorically are particularly helpful as a medium for communication with children who do not respond adequately to traditional treatment approaches. As song lyrics are a familiar, friendly medium to most children, they usually respond in a nonthreatened manner to the lyrics. Song lyrics provide the needed distance and, at the same time, articulate the child's hidden feelings, because the child can safely listen to and often discuss the situation of the person found in the lyrics. Even though the child's situation may be similar to that in the lyrics, such as feeling abandoned, unloved, or lonesome, the child is able to confront it in the context of the metaphoric lyrics, simply because it refers to "someone else." After sensorimotor maneuvers have opened up communication between the therapist and the child in Paraverbal Communication, this verbal, metaphoric use of song lyrics serves as an artifact in bridging the chasm of anxiety and mistrust, characteristic of the psychotherapeutically inaccessible child. The child is stimulated through the metaphoric use of the lyrics and so can move ahead to communicate verbally in a more traditional, specific way.

The metaphoric use of lyrics can also be used effectively with groups of children who respond to the power and safety of the metaphor and are then stimulated to communicate hidden feelings. For example, in a group of children, a therapist introduced the spiritual, "Sometimes I Feel Like a Motherless Child." She chanted the spiritual softly and emphasized the word *motherless*. The spiritual goes in part as follows:

> Sometimes I feel like a motherless child
> Sometimes I feel like a motherless child
> Sometimes I feel like a motherless child
> > A long ways from home
> > A long ways from home

At the end of this song, one usually silent girl in the class spontaneously murmured, "Yeah, that's how I feel when I come home from school every day. The room is dark and ain't nobody home." She had unconsciously used the spiritual metaphorically and, as a result, communicated for the first time her own sense of loneliness and abandonment. When the therapist said, "That's sad. It could make a child scared and even angry," other children were moved to add their own feelings to what she had communicated. There then ensued and developed not only social development through shared feelings but extended vocabulary too, i.e., sad, angry, scared, and other affective words that were added to the group's vocabulary as they spontaneously communicated.

Spirituals are particularly useful as a means of communication as are other folk and even rock song lyrics. They are useful as metaphoric bridges for the following reasons:

1. They use simple repetitive language and melodies and are easily understood by the children.
2. They are rooted in often profound and universal feelings, which capture the similar feelings of the children.
3. They are easily available on tapes or in folk song books.

The Paraverbal strategy of using metaphoric lyrics can be employed with individuals, groups, and dyads.

Song lyrics are of prime significance in Paraverbal Communication and are, although verbal, nevertheless, not identical with speech. They are a unique, pleasurable medium that combines the attractive stimuli of both rhyme and rhythm. When in addition they are used metaphorically, the union forms a viable conduit for communication by bypassing the threat inherent in ordinary dialogue. Also, when at times lyrics are used for their literal value, they provide children with additional avenues of communication. This concrete use of lyrics is described in the various chapters where they apply to the Paraverbal Communication work done with children at risk.

In the Paraverbal Communication method, communication is also facilitated through repetition, an integral part of the method in its use of sound and movement maneuvers. Repetition is present when the children join in repeatedly tapping their own rhythmic improvisations used in the sessions. Repetition is present when the children jump, stretch, stamp, or bounce a ball to repeated rhythms or when they paint or chalk rhythmically to the inherent repetitions in recorded symphonic music. Repetition is also an outstanding valuable characteristic of the folk song which is frequently used in Paraverbal Communication. In folk songs, repetition is found in many forms, including repeated melodic phrases, accent, pitch, pulse, rhythm, dynamics, and lyrics. Repetition in the lyrics is illustrated in the following example from the folk song, "Won't You Sit Down Sister?"

> (very softly) Won't you sit down Sister?
> (loudly) I can't sit down
> (very softly) Won't you sit down Sister?
> (more loudly) I can't sit down
> (very loudly) Won't you sit down Sister?
> (very loudly) I can't sit down
> Cause I just got to Heaven, gonna look around

In addition to its communicative significance, all this lyric repetition helps specifically in language and learning and can be effectively employed without fear of monotony, because contrast can be provided by the variety of components available in the sound maneuver. For example, the words *sit down* are chanted repeatedly but vary in rhythm, accent, pulse, dynamics, and pitch. This sound variation provides the contrast needed to stimulate and sustain interest.

Repetition not only intensifies communication of feelings but promotes a sense of mastery because of the many possible variations of the dynamics. Repetition makes it possible for lyrics, traditional or improvised, to be easily remembered because the previously heard lyrics are predictable. This is a boon for the child who often has difficulty with mastery. Folk songs soon mastered then become for the child what they were for their originators, a welcome, familiar means of communication.

From repetition the child appears to gain a sense of efficacy, an opportunity for sustained pleasure, and, concomitantly, a release from anxiety. Reference is made here to the anxiety a disturbed child might feel when unaware of what the child is supposed to know or supposed to do, for example, the anxiety of not knowing sequences or how to complete once started. The repetition, with its sequences of repeated pulses, rhythms, and phrases, automatically provides an opportunity for a sense of closure, of having finished. As a result, one can often observe a child's feeling of well-being, which then seems to help free the child to communicate.

Repetition also produces a most important by-product, motor education. This particular aspect of repetition is extremely important, because motor expression is part of the whole equipment of the child, including perception, cognition, and affect. Motor education, which is bound up with the child's total way of learning, develops throughout the Paraverbal maneuvers. It occurs during the on-going repetition of the child's improvisational rhythmic dialogues with the therapist. It takes place when the child tries to achieve new expressive effects, exploring new instruments of different sizes, shapes, and textures. While exploring, the child puts various body parts in rhythmic contact with the variously constructed instruments. For example, when the child hits a tambourine on his knee, he produces one kind of sound. When he scratches it with his nails or knuckles, another effect is produced. And when he raises it aloft and shakes it, still another effect if produced. Motor education, as the child changes dynamics with small or wide motions, occurs too upon repetition of the adult's rhythmic pattern, jumping, clapping, stamping, or rolling a ball rhythmically to the instrumental improvisations. Motor education continues as the child dramatizes action songs and, in a more subtle way, when he paints or chalks to symphonic records with their repeated musical components and phrases. The child is often stimulated to move not only his hands but also his body in response to various components of the music that are especially meaningful to him while he participates in this sound maneuver. For example, some children respond strongly to accent, some to dynamics, some to tempo, some to rhythmic pattern, and some to various combinations of the components of the music. Others do a limited dance before the easel, bend their knees rhythmically, or tap their feet and move their heads as they paint to the rhythmic music.

The varied and constant rhythmic motor repetition increases the ease, freedom, authority, and confidence with which children use their bodies. Their smiles and proud expressions reveal their pleasure as they work. Communication is thus further facilitated. Lauretta Bender, after observing the effectiveness of Paraverbal Communication with its consistent use of movement, among other interventions, commented on the significance of motor activity for disturbed children.

Paraverbal Communication with its sensorimotor approach and its rationale of acceptance and pleasure is useful in helping children to communicate at every level of development. Most of the Paraverbal sensorimotor materials and strategies employed in the maneuvers are of specific and practical value in each phase of the child's individual style of development. A knowledge of the characteristics of each developmental stage is important, so that the therapist can adapt the basic Paraverbal Communication maneuvers and concepts to the individual developmental needs of a particular child. Simultaneously, the child's individual atypical problems must be constantly borne in mind during the entire Paraverbal Communication involvement with the child. For the therapist to successfully achieve the desired goal of improved communication in both cognitive and behavioral areas, the therapist must know and be alert to when and for how long the Paraverbal materials and strategies are used for each individual child with his unique developmental problems. Detailed examples of different strategies are given in the specific chapters on a variety of difficulties in the cognitive and behavioral areas. These involve age levels beginning with the youngest and continuing through each phase of development, including adolescence.

An example of the strategies used can be found in the interactive maneuvers used in working with a child in the youngest group. One of the primary characteristics of this early childhood stage is the thrust toward autonomy. In developing this autonomy, the therapist must be sensitive to the child's simple, spontaneous movements, whether they be arm, finger, head, or other body part. These movements then need to be imitated by the therapist to underscore the child's autonomy. When a Paraverbal material such as a drum is used by a child, his slightest tapping movement needs to be observed and imitated too. All of these movements are immediately imitated by the therapist. One of the purposes of this imitation is to give the child concrete proof that what he originates, whether in body movement or with materials, is accepted. In this way, his developing autonomy is confirmed over and over as the therapist responds to and imitates his various movements.

The same effort toward development of autonomy is reinforced with the use of nursery songs. For example, one often used is called "Whatever I Do, Do Like Me." The therapist chants the song with appropriate motions and involves the child by encouraging the child to imitate her. Then the therapist changes to words the second time to "Whatever Johnny does, we do like Johnny" to give the child the feeling of autonomy and leadership, through the attachment of his name to his motions.

This early stage is followed by the latency stage of development. With these children, the maneuvers can become more complex. Also, attention spans are greater in these somewhat older children. There is behavioral as well as language development in the application of Paraverbal Communication, because the children not only imitate, but share materials and actions. Sharing is but one of the behavioral developments achieved through the Paraverbal techniques. Details are included in the various illustrative chapters throughout the book.

While many changes in the developmental stages of children are apparent, there is one interesting marked parallel in the developmental behavior of both the very young child and that of the adolescent. Both age level groups need or insist on autonomy. Although the need to develop autonomy is a common characteristic of both the adolescent and the young child, the wide difference in age demands more sophisticated approaches for the adolescent in both materials and technique. When working with the adolescent, the difference is apparent particularly in language development. One can observe this difference in maturity as the adolescent uses the material found in the lyrics of rock songs to communicate feelings and thoughts. The teenager translates experiences into ideas and associations. More detailed information on this aspect of autonomous adolescent communication is found in Chapter 9. Briefly, however, adolescents seize on the affective words of the lyrics. In the course of using rock lyrics, they develop their own language, often in heated group discussion of the meaning of the lyrics and their application to their own lives. In addition to this being an autonomous cognitive developmental experience, it also has a socializing effect and leads to further expanded areas of communication.

Just as there are wide variations in behavior, there are many variations in children's responses to Paraverbal Communication maneuvers at all stages of development as children interact to develop better communication. Through the variety of maneuvers, the therapist can observe the children's responses and patterns of behavior and, in this way, better assist them in their ability to communicate. For example, some children have difficulty in changing instruments or the way in which they use them. Therefore, when after a period, a child does not spontaneously seek other instruments or use the instrument in an exploratory manner, the therapist structures the situation to help the child gain in spontaneity and expressiveness, leading, of course, to better communication. The structure can be presented in many ways.

For example, with a rigid, timid child, the therapist selects a new drum. If the child is using a small one, the therapist deliberately selects a much larger drum than the one used by the child. The therapist uses it and then echoes the improvisations but somewhat louder on this new and larger percussion instrument. Thus the child is alerted to a new bridge to communication by being offered a chance to exchange instruments. Sometimes two or three instruments of larger size are put in front of the child, and when he looks interested enough, the therapist says, "Now, let's use a different instrument." If the timid child clings to his instrument and his rigid way of using it, the next step is to invite one or two more outgoing children from the class to act as participating visitors and foils for the timid child. Usually the example of the visitors' uninhibited, more pleasureful, vigorous tapping, dancing, or dramatization stimulates the timid, rigid child to imitate them. At least it encourages the child to new explorations, whether in the choice of a new instrument size or in a new use of the original instrument. To obtain spontaneity and expression, sometimes it is necessary to go even a step further in structuring the session. For example, if working with a timid child, who improvises in his or her usual manner, the therapist can turn to an outgoing visitor and tell this child to copy the child's soft pattern, only to copy it louder on the usually large instrument. Should there be a third child visiting, he can be asked to do the same thing but to increase the dynamics still further. Then the therapist can say, "Now all three of you play together." The timid child seems to gain confidence and support from playing with these more outgoing and actively participating peers as he now is provided with a means of identifying with them. Some of the viability of this activity comes from the fact that children themselves, including the timid ones, enjoy the excitement of the gradually increasing dynamics and more dramatic body movements while having the support of peers.

Paraverbal Communication can be effectively used in dyad form as well as in the one-to-one and group forms already described. With two children, it has been useful for work with shy or resistant mothers and their young children as described in Chapter 11. It has also been of significant therapeutic value in working with the abusive mother and child as described in Chapter 5. The dyad, in which another patient is used as an assistant therapist, has also been used by Heimlich to reach an inaccessible child.

In this case, two children were involved, an older girl of 13 designated as an assistant therapist to the therapist and an inaccessible elective mute 5-year-old girl with whom she worked. The older girl M was invited to help with the younger girl after the therapist noticed how tenderly she helped the youngster tie her shoes. When invited to help with this child, M was told how the young child would not speak, could not communicate, and therefore could not be helped to get better. The older girl was intrigued as she heard about the use of materials, the pleasure involved, and the acceptance of whatever the child did. Together M and the therapist planned each session. For the 13-year old, it was helpful because the experience of observing the therapist as together they strove to treat the younger child and develop her trust, which was previously lacking. She was able to observe the therapist's accepting and interested attitude both toward the child and herself.

In the course of the sessions, M was able to cope with her own hidden anger toward her parents and her brother as well as her sense of inadequacy in school and at home. This progress came about because of her joy in the materials she herself used and her delight in the responsiveness of the child with whom both she and the therapist were working. Her deep satisfaction in the communicative improvement in her young "patient" added to her sense of achievement. At the end of each session, M would offer her opinions regarding the young child's behavior and response. In the course of this interchange with the therapist, she would "interpret" what the child's angry or sad or fearful emotions were as the child communicated them through the use of materials and her own body movement. M often spontaneously used the end of session time to project many of her own problems on to her "patient." The alliance with the therapist gave her a needed sense of significance. At the same time, the nurturing, progressive work she had to employ in helping to treat the younger child automatically resulted in her using the same maneuvers, so that she could satisfy her own needs with dignity. In the course of the work, her trust in the therapist developed, because she was able to observe the therapist's accepting and interested attitude toward both the younger child and herself. Once the relationship became established, M was able to accept confrontation, which resulted in an end to her presenting problem. Her deep satisfaction in the communicative improvement in her young "patient" added to her sense of achievement and made it easier for her to communicate her own feelings to the therapist. Further details of this case as well as additional illustrations of the technique of using a child as an assistant therapist are found in Chapter 10.

In Paraverbal Communication, the therapeutic goal is to make available lines of communication appropriate for every child. For example, the sonorities and dynamics (loud, soft) of the sound maneuvers described in Chapter 3, make available a new and different line of communication. It is a unique, open channel of communication through which a child can easily communicate with an adult. The affective properties communicate something other than words to which a child can safely react. The mutual communication that can so readily take place through the use of the materials in the sound maneuvers makes the interaction between the child and the therapist an attractive, viable one for the resistant child. The sound maneuvers frequently stimulate other sensory modalities, which can also lead to communication. One of the values of the sound maneuvers is that they are an open channel for communication because the sonorities cannot be shut out. As opposed to words, sounds automatically get in. The fact that sound as an auditory sensory modality contains many different elements (tone, rhythm, pulse, dynamics, and pitch) contributes to its usefulness in developing communication. The affective properties used in the sound maneuvers send in something different from ordinary words to which the child can safely respond instead of the words the child so fears. As a unique medium of communication, the sound maneuvers provide many open and closed limits as well as selective potentials for both the therapist and the child. An example is the limits set by the size of a drum or the shape of a bell. The control and structure inherent in the various sound maneuvers provide many opportunities for the child to appropriately communicate.

Summary

Paraveral Communication is an alternate approach to communication for use with children from early childhood through adolescence, particularly for children who do not respond to traditional forms of therapy or teaching. Many of these children are withdrawn, distractible, or hyperactive, and have poor attention spans and poor self-esteem.

Basic to Paraverbal Communication is the idea that ordinary direct speech is itself threatening to many of these children. The Paraverbal multisensory interactive approach uses sound and movement maneuvers in the service of the child's moment-to-moment communicative needs. Therapeutic interaction develops spontaneously between the child and the therapist according to what is communicated.

Materials are often used metaphorically, according to the therapist's observed cues, which are gleaned from the child's behavior. The rationale for the Paraverbal Communication method is that if the child can be engaged through means that are pleasurable, the child can be made to feel accepted and to trust. Then the needed relationship for development of appropriate behavior and learning can take place. At this point, the child will be able to discharge tension, be relieved of anxiety, and communicate.

3

How and When to Apply
Specific Paraverbal Maneuvers

Nine maneuvers, or therapeutic sensorimotor interactions, were developed to provide children with ways to connect their emotional and cognitive experiences with pleasureful, metaphorically expressive media and thereby communicate. These maneuvers, which actively involve the child and the therapist, engage the child through two distinct types of simple interactions, *sound* and/or *movement*.

A child who chooses a material whose dominant property is sound, such as a drum, has the choice of expressing himself with any one or combination of the many elements in sound, such as loud and soft intensities, fast and slow tempos, and self-generated rhythms or accents that can vitalize his actions. One Paraverbal use of sound that engages children readily and encourages them to respond is chanting with its playful rhyme and rhythms so familiar to chil-

41

dren. This pleasureful nonthreatening manner of communicating by both the child and the therapist stimulates children to make up additional descriptive chanting phrases. The use of chanting to accompany their actions enables children to communicate more readily than they could with direct speech alone.

Other children may be attracted by a material that predominantly involves movement. Some children are overly sensitive to sound and prefer to communicate through movement. Paraverbal Communication is able to provide communicative channels for such children through specific movement maneuvers. For example, rather than choosing a sound-producing percussion instrument, a child may pick up a lump of clay and begin to roll or squeeze it. The child responds tactilely to the texture, and the moldable clay changes shape. The child can experience immediately how the clay responds to his touch and feelings. Through this type of movement experience, even a timid child can quickly realize his own efficacy.

Sound and movement experiences each contribute in their own way to feelings of raised self-esteem in children. The maneuvers foster these experiences and permit the therapist to readily join the child in therapeutic development. Through this interaction, the therapist finds herself in the unique position of being both a participant and an observer in the maneuvers as she can respond actively and therapeutically to the child's behavioral cues.

Communication develops through two types of participation, *synchronous* and *reciprocal*. In synchronous or simultaneous interaction, the child and the therapist interact simultaneously using percussive instruments, other Paraverbal materials, or movement maneuvers. When using percussion instruments in synchronous interaction, a child is encouraged to tap and chant his name. The therapist can illustrate if necessary in order to involve the child. The child taps, *John*-ny. The therapist then imitates his tapping and simultaneously chants his name, *John*-ny, with strong emphasis on the first syllable of the name. The therapist might now suggest that they tap and chant the name simultaneously a few times—*John*-ny, *John*-ny, *John*-ny—so that the child experiences the pleasure of having his name made special by both the therapist and himself. A prime value to the child of this tapping interaction is the immediacy of response with its accompanying pleasure and sense of satisfaction.

In a reciprocal rhythmic tapping exchange, the participants alternate their tapping responses, which constitute a dialogue, and, through their reciprocal interaction, the nonverbal dialogue is completed. For example, the child may tap and chant his two-syllable first name, *John*-ny; the therapist would complete the phrase by tapping and chanting his one-syllable last name, *Jones.* They then repeat this 3-syllable name phrase, *John*-ny *Jones, John*-ny *Jones, John*-ny *Jones* in a reciprocal manner with each doing his part. In addition to providing pleasure, the repetition and compelling rhythmic pattern also produce mastery. Interacting either synchronously or reciprocally, the child experiences typical Paraverbal acceptance and pleasure.

Imitation, employed frequently in the synchronous and reciprocal maneuvers, is a significant strategy in Paraverbal Communication because of its therapeutic and cognitive effects. When the therapist imitates the child, this action validates what the child is doing and immediately makes him feel he's doing something right. Then, when the child imitates the therapist, the child also feels he's doing what is called for and experiences the needed sense of achievement. This imitating interaction often marks a beginning of the child's identification with the therapist. As for the cognitive aspect, the imitation inherent in the Paraverbal maneuvers provides needed basic learning experiences. A child learns more effectively through his own active involvement in the maneuvers because of the pleasurable reciprocal or synchronous interaction with the therapist in which imitation plays a large part.

The specific problems and emotional needs of each child suggest to the therapist which maneuver or combination of maneuvers can most effectively address those needs. Children referred for attention deficits, aggressivity, withdrawn behavior, anxiety, learning difficulties, or other childhood communication difficulties respond to Paraverbal Communication because the materials and maneuvers immediately begin to address their specific needs. For example, an inattentive child can be quickly engaged by the unique sounds of percussive instruments. The child's interest and attention are maintained by tapping rhythmic patterns and improvising new ways of tapping them. Different tempos and intensities of tapping can be introduced, for example, fast, then slow. After this, the therapist can introduce loud and then soft tapping, thereby giving the child many varieties of organizing and communicating experiences that keep the child interested and involved. By observing the child's unique use of the materials and his improvisations, the therapist can better understand which maneuvers will further the child's growth. For example, if a child becomes overly stimulated by a large drum (a sound maneuver), the therapist would substitute a quieter maneuver, dominated by movement rather than sound, for example, a maneuver that uses clay. The child can still discharge tension by cutting or hitting the clay, and this metaphoric use of the clay will also maintain the child's attention. The typical Paraverbal metaphoric use of materials in all the maneuvers allows the child to ventilate feelings safely. The resultant achievement of emotional relief, feelings of acceptance, safety in communicating emotions, and the pleasure that children have using the materials suggested in the maneuvers encourage them to want to repeat the experiences.

Children quickly learn to improvise and explore new ways of using the materials based upon their preferences and needs. Through this freedom of exploration, the child gains even more ways of communicating. Some children find new effects spontaneously. Other children need to be encouraged. Children often want to use the same materials in different ways. For example, a child might use a drum to tap his name, then dramatize anger on the same drum. Another child might choose different materials to create similar therapeutic experiences for himself. He might use the cymbals to dramatize sadness and then communicate a similar feeling using castanets, drum, or other instrument. He might even spontaneously choose a puppet to dramatize his sadness. The sounds of the different instruments and the evocative materials often stimulate the child to communicate many other feelings. In the process, children can achieve desired therapeutic states, such as improved self-esteem and the ability to trust.

As therapists become familiar with the maneuvers and their specific communicative therapeutic efficacy, they can begin to improvise their own ways to utilize the materials to facilitate each child's specific therapeutic journey. Children suffer many different types of deficits. There are also children who suffer similar deficits but for different reasons. The Paraverbal maneuvers are structured to address the many types of deficits with therapeutic interaction appropriate to each child's needs. When mental health professionals understand how, when, and why to use specific maneuvers, their own therapeutic training and experience will then reinforce their ability to more accurately choose the maneuvers that can best help each child, according to his need.

Each maneuver can be flexibly manipulated by the therapist for a variety of goals. For example, sometimes sound is used to enable the child to discharge tension; at other times, sound is used to gain attention. Many different maneuvers can produce therapeutic results, such as improved self-esteem, ventilation of feelings, ability to trust, and impulse control, but the therapist will choose the specific maneuver depending upon the child's need. For example, if the objective is to have the child experience improved self-esteem, a child can tap a pattern, or imitate the therapist, or be imitated by the therapist, or blow a soap bubble into the air and then break it, or guess what feeling the therapist is dramatizing with the cymbals. All of these interactions enable the child to feel more confident and competent. The decision of which specific maneuver to use will be determined by many factors, such as the individual child's needs, his preferences in materials, his emotional state (aggressive or withdrawn), and what has already taken place in the sessions.

All of the maneuvers are geared toward communication to aid learning and changing inappropriate behavior. Chapters 5–12 illustrate the use of the maneuvers to address specific presenting problems. The same rationale for engaging individual children with the materials and maneuvers applies when using Paraverbal Communication with children in small groups. Chapters 6, 10, and 11 illustrate uses of the maneuvers with more than one child.

The following maneuvers (1–9) provide instructive illustrations of Paraverbal Communication. With an awareness of the rationale underlying each maneuver and the Paraverbal techniques for interacting with the child, the therapist has the basis for needed therapeutic and cognitive interventions and communication.

The maneuvers are numbered beginning with the simplest and progressing to more complex in order to satisfy the burgeoning emotional needs of the child. The maneuvers make accessible to the child a variety of communicative channels for meeting his evolving needs. Once the therapeutic possibilities inherent in each maneuver are understood, the therapist can use them in any order to respond to any change a child initiates.

Maneuver 1:
A Simple Rhythmic Dialogue to Begin the Relationship

In this first maneuver, the therapist makes available to the child a few percussion instruments of varying size and shape such as a tambourine, drums, or castanets. A child is free to choose whichever instrument appeals to him. The great value of the child choosing the medium through which to communicate is that the child becomes especially motivated to act upon what he himself has chosen. The therapist does not need to spend time trying to convince the child to participate. Instead, the therapist reacts therapeutically to the child by beginning to improvise with these accepted communicative tools to address the child's problems.

A timid child is likely to choose a small instrument. An aggressive child is likely to select a large one. Their choices often reflect their needs, and they usually begin to explore the instruments immediately by spontaneously tapping out a simple rhythmic pattern such as $-\cdot-$, $-\cdot-$. As soon as the child makes this personal improvisation, the therapist recognizes it by imitating it on the instrument she believes to be appropriate at the moment.

If a child has difficulty choosing an instrument, the therapist models the behavior for him by enthusiastically choosing one first, then offering the child one and inviting him to tap a pattern on it. If the child does not spontaneously tap a pattern, the therapist can model the behavior. The child need not choose a percussion instrument. This tapping maneuver is generally the first offered because of its easy-to-follow structure and simplicity.

Depending upon the child's response to this point, the therapist is prepared to interact with the child. If the child chooses a drum and taps a rhythmic pattern, the therapist imitates that rhythmic pattern. If the child chooses a drum but does not initiate a pattern, the therapist can encourage the child by gesturing for him to imitate her pattern. They thereby begin a rhythmic dialogue. If the child chooses a different material, the therapist responds by using the appropriate Paraverbal maneuvers to interact with the child.

Once the child and the therapist are involved in rhythmic dialogue, however simple, the therapist can then begin to incorporate variations into the first maneuver. These variations sustain interest, address the child's behavioral needs, and provide for additional learning and a sense of achievement. The following variations are only a few of many possibilities:

1. Tapping variations of the patterns—loud and then soft; fast and then slow
2. Tapping the pattern 2 times, then 3 times, according to the child's needs
3. Tapping out in syllables the names of the child, the therapist, friends, family members, or others, and changing the names to accompany the rhythmic tapping, e.g., *John*-ny *Ap*-ple-seed, Al-ex-*an*-der *Jones*
4. Chanting an improvised lyric to accompany the pattern, e.g., I like *John*-ny, yes I *do* to the tune of the familiar song, *Frère Jacques*
5. Using alternate methods of producing the sound, e.g., using knuckles, nails, back of hand, or fist to produce patterns
6. Clapping rhythmic patterns, snapping fingers, stamping feet while remaining seated
7. Standing and stamping the patterns, walking around the room, slowly at first, then fast; on tiptoe, then full foot
8. Taking turns directing each other to tap patterns loud and soft by slowly moving hands upward for loud and downward for soft—the therapist models the directing motion for the child who taps the drum based on her cues; then the child moves his hands to cue the therapist

It is important that therapists feel at ease using the first maneuver with a child before moving to the other maneuvers. If the therapist feels at ease and enjoys using the materials, the child will generally respond in the same way and be eager to try new materials and activities often at the therapist's suggestion. All other maneuvers employ different materials in a variety of ways, but the nonthreatening manner of introducing them through the child's choices is always the same.

Maneuver 2: Metaphoric Statement of Feelings

Now that the child is more familiar and at ease with the materials and pleasurable maneuvers, he will generally welcome the opportunity to choose other materials and participate. Even though the child has first choice in selecting materials to use, there are times when the therapist needs to introduce a specific communicative tool to meet a current need. For example, the therapist may offer the child a pair of large cymbals and say, "Show me any feeling you want to—anger, fear, sadness, or any other feeling. Show it with your cymbals and show the feeling on your face. I will try to guess your feeling and you tell me if I am right." The child will generally be eager to participate and nearly always will comment on whether the therapist guessed right or wrong. If the child hesitates, the therapist models this dramatization of the feeling and asks the child to guess her feeling. The child learns quickly from observing. Now, the therapist can say, "We'll take turns," and then signals for the child to dramatize. The therapist guesses. If the therapist has guessed correctly, she can hazard to ask, "When might people feel this way?" If she is incorrect, she can ask the child to repeat the dramatization and offer her a verbal cue. Usually this brings the appropriate response. Sometimes, to clarify a child's feeling, the therapist can ask the child to show, with the large cymbals and on his face, the opposite feeling of one just dramatized.

The ventilation of feelings generally leads to a beginning discussion about these troublesome feelings and the
child's problem. Additionally, vocabulary is developed to
communicate these feelings. Large cymbals are most effective for enabling the child to ventilate feelings. However, the
child could also choose a tambourine or drum on which to
dramatize and still be effective.

Maneuver 3: Metaphoric Use of String Instruments

Several kinds of instruments can be used with this maneuver, including the autoharp, a flat horizontal stringed instrument, and the guitar. Children enjoy using the autoharp
because it produces a loud, rich, string sound. No previous
experience is necessary for using an autoharp as employed
in this maneuver. A guitar can be used if an autoharp is not
available. This maneuver will be explained using the autoharp, because it possesses additional therapeutic benefits
other than its sound alone.

The autoharp is placed across the laps of both the child
and the therapist as they face each other knee to knee. This
positioning of the instrument immediately creates a sharing
relationship and face to face interaction between child and
the therapist. The therapist offers the child a strumming
stick and tells him to strum while she plays the chords. The
chord buttons, on which the chords are clearly marked, only
need to be individually pressed down to automatically produce a pleasant harmonious sound. The therapist can strum
a loud sound and show the child how to silence the strings
by placing his hands across them. Children derive great
pleasure from the silencing power of their action. If necessary, the therapist can demonstrate for the child by strumming loudly across strings and then silencing them with her
hand. The child often asks to press the chord buttons and
strum while the therapist silences the strings. There are

many interactive variations for using this maneuver. What is important is that the child experiences the pleasure of producing and silencing the sound at will. This maneuver has many metaphoric uses. If the child is timid, the therapist can present the loud strumming sound metaphorically as "children making noise" and request that the child tell them to "be quiet" by silencing the strings with his hands. The child generally does just that, silences the strings and says, "Be quiet!" The variations of this use of the autoharp are endless. The child's specific problems will indicate how the therapist can improvise effective ways to address them.

Another distinct metaphoric use of the autoharp or guitar permits a child to identify family members and friends by plucking individual strings. For example, a child might loudly pluck a deep, low string to produce a "father" sound, and a soft, high string for "mother." A child may identify all family members except himself or he may exclude a member. These sound messages convey significant information about the child's personal perceptions of himself, his family, or other relationships, and can generate much therapeutic discussion.

Maneuver 4: Metaphoric Statements of Feelings

This maneuver acts as a bridge so children can safely ventilate feelings and ideas and connect these feelings to the specificities of words. Children are stimulated by the unique and novel properties of the Paraverbal materials to ventilate feelings, not only in a single word but complete thoughts and sentences such as, "I hate school" or "I hate _____ (person)." The metaphoric use of the instruments provides the needed distance to make the child feel safe in revealing otherwise hidden and often forbidden thoughts. The child can then move to the next step.

This maneuver is usually a therapeutic outgrowth of a

previous interaction or maneuver. For example, a child might have just dramatized anger using the cymbals (Maneuver 2) and safely talked about people's angry feelings. At this point, the therapist could lead him on and suggest he show these "mad" feelings using the drum by placing it in front of him. One child hit the drum loud and rhythmically and then felt free to say, "I hate ____" (his brother who was the cause of much of the child's distress). This revelation was the beginning of the child's therapy and growth. Another child, after dramatizing fear using the cymbals, picked up the castanets and began to click them together. In response to the therapist's stating that a person feels alone when he is scared, the child clicked the castanets and chanted, "I'm scared of Daddy." This revealing statement led to further discussion about specific fears and the issue could be addressed. This maneuver provided many opportunities to safely ventilate this child's fears and achieve an improved level of functioning.

The child's metaphoric statements can always be intensified or further defined through loud, soft, fast, or slow adaptations. These subtle variations permit a child to approach threatening feelings with less anxiety than might be the case if directly spoken. For example, a child might feel more comfortable at first softly and tentatively tapping and chanting the hidden thought and only later feel more at ease tapping and stating it loudly. The Paraverbal maneuvers provide these needed concrete channels to communicate what should not be hidden but cannot immediately be verbally revealed.

Through rhythmic song stories using percussion instruments to intensify his story, a child can communicate feelings, choose instruments on which to communicate and underscore these feelings, and make personal decisions about the story. Children obtain great pleasure as they create many unique sound effects that enhance and enliven their storytelling. The therapist begins, "Once there was a boy..." and waits for the child to add whatever he chooses, perhaps a boy, a dog, or a monster. To underscore what the child is telling, a variety of percussion instruments are available for him to intensify and communicate the moods of the story. For example, a monster might be characterized by a loud thump on a drum; a boy might be indicated by a simple tap, tap, tap of a drum. Running sounds can be created by tapping the fingertips rapidly on a drum. Within the safety of this technique, a child may reveal particular feelings and want to use an instrument in the way he thinks can best communicate his ideas. For example, a child may say, "Now the boy is afraid," and will use the instrument he thinks can best communicate that fear. The therapist should praise the child for his unique use of the instruments and encourage him to continue.

Maneuver 5:
Rhythmic Movement with Chanted Accompaniment

Through the movement interactions in Maneuver 5, a child learns about himself in relation to space and to other persons. The child also learns by observing the therapist's use of her own hands, arms, and feet, and by other body movements. This meaningful involvement results in the child's pleasurable movement with the materials and desire to continue to use them. During this pleasurable interaction, the therapist can harness a child's compulsive motions (if evident) into therapeutic, rhythmic, and purposeful motions. If the child is merely timid, this maneuver readily engages the child by providing modeling by the therapist and chanting that indicates to the child "how to." For example, the pleasure of walking on the plastic cups, pulling rope, tapping cymbals together, throwing and catching a nerf ball, or rolling or bouncing a ball, all to descriptive rhythmic accompaniment encourages a child to fully participate and, in the process, experience pleasure, mastery, and communication.

There are many creative therapeutic possibilites for involving children through movement. For example, a timid child may find it difficult to spontaneously initiate an active or large body movement. However, the therapist can hand one end of a rope to the child and begin to rhythmically and gently pull and simultaneously chant, "Pulling, pulling back and forth." The child will generally reciprocate and pull within the rhythmic structure because of the pleasure it brings. Once the child is engaged in the maneuver, the therapist can suggest variations; for example, the child could also chant the song. The therapist can then suggest that they change the tempo of their pulling song, by pulling slowly at first and then rapidly after the therapist gives the cue. This novel change, even though announced, brings heightened pleasure to the child and further encourages the child to participate. Finally, the therapist can encourage the child to change the tempo in order to surprise the therapist. Being in control in this way, the child experiences increased self-esteem and resultant pleasure.

In another variation of this movement maneuver, a child blows soap bubbles and can catch them on a cymbal, smash them, or act upon them in any chosen manner that enables the child to ventilate his feelings. A child will often attach names (of family members or friends) to the bubbles. For example, a small bubble might represent a baby brother and a large bubble, the father. Through the therapist's chanted accompaniment identifying the child's movements, the child can work through situations.

A copying song encourages a child to participate. The therapist tells the child, "We're going to sing a copying song called 'Whatever I Do, Do Like Me,'" and improvises this song, "Whatever I do, do like me," and claps her hands for her motion. The therapist can motion the child to do the same and continue with the song and a different motion such as stamping her foot. To involve the child, the therapist then sings, "Whatever John does, I'll do like John does," and then waits for the child to make his motion. As soon as the child makes any gesture, the therapist copies it and continues this maneuver until the child has achieved the needed discharge of tension and satisfaction of being the leader and participating reciprocally.

With a young child, the therapist might sit on the floor and roll a ball back and forth to the child while chanting a descriptive message, "We roll the ball back and forth." The pleasurable interaction of ball rolling and chanting engages the child, and the therapist can then begin to involve the child in improvising new motions and words.

Maneuver 6:
Psychomotor Rhythmic Body Movement and Role Playing

This dynamic maneuver can be therapeutically useful after the previous movement maneuver. The child generally has experienced the needed discharge of tension and feels at ease using the materials in new ways to communicate feelings. This maneuver gives the child further opportunity to be in an active and assertive but playful interaction with the therapist who acts as the model in a cymbal dialogue.

The child and the therapist sit facing each other and each holds one cymbal. The child is given the choice of large or small cymbals. After the child chooses, the therapist takes the matching cymbal and with large motions, gently taps the child's cymbal while simultaneously providing descriptive cues through a chant, "I hit John and John hits me." The child generally follows the cues and continues to follow them. Tempo and intensity variations can be added immediately according to the needs of the child. "I hit softly

and John hits softly." "I hit hard and John hits hard." "We
hit softly." "We hit fast." The child generally offers suggestions and is delighted to see his ideas used and validated.
The slow–fast and loud–soft variations reinforce previous experiences in other maneuvers and add to the child's sense of
mastery.

At this point, the therapist can introduce any improvisation that addresses the child's problem. For example, in
the case of sibling rivalry, the therapist can suggest that she
role-play Billy, the younger brother. If the child agrees, the
therapist chants, "I hit Billy and Billy hits me." The child
will usually provide his own improvisations and may suggest they do it hard or other variations that permit him to
safely ventilate his feelings. The structure of the maneuver
includes small or large cymbals and a variety of verbal ac-
companiments as rhythmic descriptive chants in a seated
position and provides opportunities for the child to discharge angry feelings safely and feel accepted. The child is
further helped by the maneuver's built-in incentive to wait
for cues. By waiting for his turn to tap, the child gets his
own chance to tap and to make choices regarding how to
tap. Therefore, impulse control is developed through the dynamic interaction centered on the child's problem, but addressed safely through metaphor. This introductory use of
metaphor now leads smoothly to the following maneuver,
which expands the use of metaphor with still other materials.

Maneuver 7: Metaphoric Use of Materials

The goal of this movement maneuver is to give the child
an opportunity to communicate through fantasies and
themes attached to concrete materials, as well as through
lyrics that describe his actions. The child thereby can ventilate feelings safely through these concrete experiences.

The wide variety of novel yet therapeutic materials available in this maneuver often suggests to the child roles he might be able to assume to discharge tension over a specific anxiety-providing situation. The free use of materials encourages and stimulates the child to communicate.

Some of the materials appropriate for this maneuver are as follows:

- Water play containers (plastic cups, lids, spoons, funnels, and other common kitchen objects)
- Soap flakes, which can be used to create foam
- Clay, paper cups, and pine cones that can be smashed

For example, the therapist chants permission to break an appropriate object such as a pine cone, "When I'm very angry, I like to break something." The child can stamp the pine cone and achieve emotional release through a discharge of anger. This way of using the maneuver is often therapeutic for a child who needs to actively and acceptably discharge aggression or reveal feelings. By observing the child, the therapist thus gains additional insight into the child's problem and obtains indications on how to further proceed with the maneuvers.

Maneuver 8: Metaphoric Use of Song Lyrics

Song lyrics are a particularly helpful medium for communication with young children and adolescents because of the pleasure they bring and the relevance of lyrics to their situations (see Chapter 9). The pleasure derived from the rhyme and rhythm of song lyrics makes this medium for communication attractive and less threatening than direct speech. The lyrics provide a needed, safe, intervening distance between the therapist and the child, as well as between the child and his own anxiety-provoking feelings.

With songs as stimuli, children have many channels for communicating feelings, including singing, dramatization, accompaniment on percussive instruments, discussion of specific song phrases and song content, and creative word changes for songs they improvise.

Lyrics can be used to nurture a child, encourage movement, deal with specific feelings, discuss a moral issue, or simply to mirror the child's feelings or activities. The lyrics may come from nursery rhymes, folk songs, or from rock and other popular music. Frequently it is valuable to improvise lyrics to specifically address a child's particular issues.

There are many ways to use song lyrics metaphorically to meet the individual needs of children. Songs with themes that parallel situations in the life of the child are chosen. After the child has heard the song lyrics and accompanied the therapist on an instrument such as the autoharp, this parallelism is often enough to encourage the child to talk about the song's story and then perhaps his own. It may be necessary to use another song with a similar theme or repeat this song to stimulate discussion. The therapist will have to observe the behavioral cues of the child for an indication of how to proceed. By identifying with the situation in a song's lyrics, a child is often able to express feelings and thoughts that might be too anxiety-provoking if he were to speak them directly.

Many folk songs relate to aggression and can be used to elicit discussion about specific issues. For example, "The Golden Vanity" is a ballad about the sinking of an enemy ship and the betrayal and death of a cabin boy; "Drill Ye Tarriers Drill" is a song that deals with blasting and a tough boss; "Waltzing Matilda" is a song about theft and death.

If the therapist wants to stimulate a child to talk about home, she might select an excerpt about home from the folk song, "Swing Low, Sweet Chariot," "coming for to carry me home." When merely spoken, the word home does not have nearly the impact on the child that it can have when wedded to the music. Set to music, the word can be sung louder than the other words and therefore it gets more attention. Another folk song, "Home on the Range," can also be used to elicit discussion about home.

The theme of rejection might be addressed with the song, "Sometimes I Feel Like a Motherless Child." With some children it may be necessary to present many folk songs with similar themes to get them to articulate their feelings. A child may simply request a song over and over, in this way, demonstrating his need and the song's potential for meeting that need. Each child will respond to the metaphoric use of lyrics in his own way. Sometimes ventilation takes place, sometimes historical material comes up, and often insight is gained.

Maneuver 9: Rhythmic Chalking
or Finger Painting to Accented Recorded Music

This maneuver provides opportunities for the child to put something of his own creation on paper and thereby communicate. Rhythmic chalkings and finger paintings are nonrepresentational, and judgment regarding good or bad productions does not enter into the experience. Each child's creation is unique. Sound and movement are integrated in this maneuver as the accented music inspires each child to produce different visual effects. A child often moves his whole body rhythmically as he chalks to the music, resulting in a release of tension in addition to pleasure.

Materials that are needed for this maneuver include an easel to which is clipped a piece of 16 × 24 black construction paper and a box of 1 × 1 thick colored pastel chalk placed near the easel. A strongly rhythmic song such as "Stars and Stripes Forever," "Waltz of the Toreadors," or Peer Gynt's

"Stormy Night" is used. The child is invited to listen to the music and rhythmically move his hands in the air. He is told to close his eyes and see what colors come to mind as he moves. Then after a minute, he is told to open his eyes, choose whatever color chalk he wants and, at the word "Go" begin moving with chalk on the paper. He is encouraged to make any free spontaneous strokes he desires. Total freedom of expression in response to any or all of the components of music, such as intensity, tempo, pitch, or general feeling, is encouraged. The therapist encourages the child to change colors, and cues him to listen for loud or soft, fast or slow in the music. The therapist can also chant and tap the rhythmic beat on the side of the easel to assist the child or can join the child in chalking on the other side of the easel. Cues gained from the child as he chalks will indicate what the child is communicating and suggest the role of the therapist in this maneuver.

When the record is over, the therapist praises the child for his creation, which is unique. There is no other chalking like it and this fact should be told to the child. Both the therapist and the child can discuss the child's chalking or both chalkings if the therapist has produced one. Emphasis should be placed on the uniqueness of each.

Chalking to music has a diagnostic as well as a therapeutic value. A study of thousands of drawings done by children shows a clear diagnostic pattern. Children who consistently use tiny delicate strokes reveal anxiety. Those who favor broad large strokes are generally aggressive and often destructive. Repetitive straight strokes usually reveal compulsiveness and rigidity. The muse of many bright colors usually shows imagination. There are many other revealing variations in the way children chalk that can be useful in helping the therapist to understand the behavior of the child, which may not be so evident or specific under ordinary classroom or therapeutic circumstances.

Summary

Through the use of the nine Paraverbal maneuvers, the therapist provides the child with a variety of sensorimotor interventions through which the child can experience pleasure, ventilate feelings, and communicate. With the therapeutic possibilities inherent in each maneuver, the therapist has at her command the basis for needed therapeutic and cognitive interventions and communication.

4

Diagnostic Assessment through Paraverbal Communication

The Need for an Auditory–Motor Percussion Test to Reveal Hidden Neurological Damage

There is an urgent need to accurately understand a child's deviant behavior and its significance as early as possible. A child's frustration caused by unmet educational and emotional needs can contribute to a host of dysfunctional behavior patterns. It was to help fulfill such needs that Heimlich (1972) designed the Auditory–Motor Percussion test. Mental health professionals often observe a child's overactivity, distractibility, impulsiveness, or aggressiveness and note the generally poor social interactional abilities and resultant underachievement. This type of underachievement and inappropriate behavior is frequently attributed to emotional disturbance or other factors unrelated to the child's physiological or neurological state. The confusion only becomes exacerbated as the child passes from grade to grade, but does not develop and progress, through school. Endless hours of testing, remediation, parent meetings, therapy, and frustration often accompany the child in school and, frequently, out of school as well.

A child exhibiting any of the above behaviors may very well have an emotional disturbance that requires a specific therapeutic environment and strategies appropriate to the child's emotional and educational development. However, children can exhibit similar deviant behavior that is not due primarily to emotional disturbance. Rather, these children may be wrestling with conditions over which they have little control. They may suffer from hidden neurological damage and therefore be unable to respond appropriately to the oral demands of the traditional classroom. When children with neurological damage are placed in inappropriate classes, they can become distractible, overactive, or withdrawn, due to frustration. These children require a classroom environment that is not dependent upon oral teaching, because they cannot adequately absorb oral instructions and information, even as presented in "traditional" special education classes. For these children, information needs to be presented through a variety of sensorimotor approaches that utilize the child's intact senses rather than frustrate the child by concentrating upon the less efficient auditory channel. The educational and social implications of failing to address a neurologically affected child are considerable and the unfortunate results to the child's intellectual and social development can be extremely damaging.

This chapter discusses a simple auditory–motor percussion test that was designed to distinguish children who show this type of neurological impairment from those who do not. The test provides an immediate alert to possible hidden neurological dysfunction in children. It is not meant to comprehensively assess central nervous system functioning.

Rather, the test is meant to reveal specific significant hidden impairment that has not come to light during the course of traditional assessment. The Auditory-Motor Percussion Test is especially effective with children over 4 years of age who have communication difficulties and for whom ordinary diagnostic tests are inadequate. An advantage of the Auditory-Motor Percussion Test is that it can be effectively administered to any child, regardless of the attendant experiences due to socioeconomic situation. The test is not dependent upon previous learning or language facility but upon the ability to process auditory rhythmic tonal patterns. With the recent increase in referrals of Hispanic children for educational underachievement (Gartner and Lipsky 1987, Canino et al. 1980), such a test may be a valuable first step in screening for hidden neurological deficits that could interfere with a child's learning. Jansky and de Hirsch (1972) point out, for example, that predictive instruments suitable for Spanish-speaking children are practically nonexistent. The Auditory–Motor Percussion Test is easy to administer by classroom teachers or mental health professionals, takes very little time compared to the two or more hours required for most neurological testing, and results are known immediately since the examiner has only to observe whether or not the child can reproduce the presented rhythmic patterns.

How the Auditory–Motor Percussion Test Serves as an Alert to Neurological Damage

The present test was developed in the course of using a rhythmic percussion dialogue as part of Paraverbal Communication therapy (Heimlich 1972) to involve inaccessible emotionally disturbed children (see Chapter 2). The Auditory–Motor Percussion Test does not seem like a test to a child since only pleasure-producing materials are used. No pen-

cils, paper, or other materials associated with the tensions of
the classroom are used. Therefore, children generally become involved in the rhythmic tapping task with playful
enthusiasm and pleasure. Within this nonthreatening atmosphere, children are free of anxiety and can reveal both their
strengths and weaknesses. In this test, children have their
choice of a variety of percussion instruments, which represent symbols of pleasure. This opportunity for a child to
choose from pleasurable materials gives him a feeling of being in command and more secure when being tested, rather
than being in a threatening test situation.

The child's attention is maintained by the novelty and
variety of the sounds of the percussion instruments and
the opportunities for changing instruments at any time.
Through the novelty, pleasure, and flexibility inherent in the
Auditory–Motor Percussion Test, children are stimulated to
participate and therefore are able to perform in the most revealing manner.

As part of this Paraverbal approach, the therapist begins
the Auditory–Motor Percussion Test by encouraging the
child to produce a simple rhythmic tonal pattern on a drum
or another available percussion instrument while she sits opposite him and enthusiastically copies his rhythm on her instrument. Together they then play his rhythm loud or soft,
fast or slow, for about a minute. Then, roles are reversed.
The therapist improvises a rhythm, which the child copies.

In the course of using this rhythmic percussion dialogue technique repeatedly in Paraverbal Communication
sessions, it was observed that some children could not accurately imitate the therapist's rhythmic patterns. The significance of this inability to imitate rhythmic patterns was
inadvertently revealed by hospital staff working with a different small group of hospitalized inaccessible children.
These children were not able to be adequately tested by
standard neurological procedures. What provoked the interest of the staff was the fact that none of the children in this

group of poorly functioning children were able to imitate rhythmic patterns in the Auditory–Motor Percussion Test. Because of the inherent value for future assessment of this difficult population, the hospital staff immediately urged further research with larger numbers of children.

Rationale for Testing

The results of a normative study of 144 children tested in settings for the normal child and 84 in settings for disturbed children supports the hypothesis that the presence of structural dysfunction in the central nervous system is probable if a child is unable to reproduce a rhythmic pattern (Heimlich 1975). The testing was based upon findings of other researchers (e.g. Luria 1966, Chalfont and Scheffelin 1969, Jansky and de Hirsch 1972, and Birch, 1964) whose works relating to auditory processing and intellectual and behavioral functioning are cited in this chapter. For example, Luria (1966) conducted similar rhythmic tapping tests in his research on adults with brain injuries and found that "the audiomotor coordination can be affected by disturbance either from defective acoustic analysis or defective motor organization." Although healthy subjects reproduced tapping without difficulty, those with neurological interference had difficulty reproducing the simple patterns. Furthermore, in the course of his research, Luria found that individuals who have suffered brain damage to frontotemporal regions of the brain had impaired rhythmic functions. He hypothesized that short-term memory functions of the frontotemporal region help account for this difficulty in reproducing rhythmic patterns. Chalfont and Scheffelin (1969) discuss deficient auditory memory and related the implications of this deficit to the classroom. They suggest that "a child who is unable to analyze a series of sounds into their separate parts or to synthesize separate sounds into wholes, may suffer impaired auditory memory, speech, and reading ability." Jansky and de Hirsch (1972) believe that tracking and auditory sequencing, auditory memory span, and auditory discrimination are crucial for the reading task. Eaves et al. (1972) state that "the faulty organization of perception and motor processes interferes with reading, writing, and arithmetic and leads to difficulties of conceptualization and symbolic learning." The early research of Stamback (1951) indicated that the "ability to imitate a series of tapped patterns was related to reading competence." Although these and other researchers recognize the importance and relevance of auditory processing to intellectual functioning, most of them note the paucity of needed research in this area. Of equal importance is the need for practical techniques for effectively assessing anxious unresponsive children. The Auditory–Motor Percussion Test is a valuable and needed addition for the complete and accurate assessment of noncommunicating children with hidden neurological damage.

Problems in Testing Children

Various investigators have reported the problems encountered when testing noncommunicating emotionally disturbed children using standard tests. They stressed the need for a wider range of tests than was available. Smith (1969) points out that "It is difficult to establish a definite diagnosis of organicity for psychiatric admission." One source of this difficulty is the fact that children with neurological and/or emotional difficulties often show similar or identical signs and symptoms. Gardner (1979) concurs and states that most examiners believe these same symptoms (hyperactivity, impulsivity, and concentration impairment) can be psychogenic in etiology or manifestations of neurological impairment. Psychogenic factors such as tension, fear, anger, and general resistance often result from anxiety due to fear of failure. Gardner continues, "anxiety reduces concentration and when attention is impaired every test result must be suspect." When intelligence testing is administered to children suffering neurological interference, anxiety is the frequent result because these children often cannot process questions nor respond appropriately. Berko (1969) mentions such symptoms as "distractibility, drifting attention, or the inability to follow through with a simple activity." He goes on to say that these symptoms are noted not only in some brain-damaged children but also in those with "severe emotional disturbances...and in many chronically ill children of various etiologies." Birch (1964), Myklebust (1954), and Belmont et al. (1969) comment on the difficulty of testing such children and note that the usefulness of available tests for them is limited.

Tapping Tests

Many researchers have used tapping tests to ascertain ability to process sound, including finger tapping tests about which Reitan (1970), Reitan and Boll (1971), Reitan and Fitzburgh (1971), Reitan et al. (1971), and Boll and Reitan (1972) have written extensively. In addition, there were those of Stevens et al.(1967), the Knox cube text (Minski 1957), and the Rudnick et al. tapping test (1967). Halstead (1947) described work with an auditory stimulus test. Although many of these tests do reveal neurological damage, the presence of such neurological impairment is not always revealed in certain children who become anxious and unresponsive in the traditional formality of most tapping test settings.

Luria, who developed a rhythmic tapping test, felt that patients' inability to reproduce a given rhythm accurately was of diagnostic neurological significance. Luria went on to say, "This aspect of investigation has unfortunately been neglected in clinical practice, but it is of very great importance in the topical diagnosis of brain lesions." The great value of Luria's research can be seen in the attempts to replicate his assessment methods. Christensen (1975) organized Luria's methods into a test battery and Golden further refined the techniques into a standardized battery for children 8 to 12 years in 1983. The Luria-Nebraska Neuropsychological Battery-Children's includes an acousticomotor organization (rhythm) subtest to measure auditory perception, discrimination, and reproduction of sounds and rhythmic patterns. However, the rigid format of many of these tests is frequently so threatening to some children that the tests do not serve their function, which is to reveal hidden neurological damage.

Procedure for Auditory–Motor Percussion Test

Percussion instruments, a small table, and two chairs for the participants are the only materials required. Several instruments of different sizes and materials, although not essential, are recommended to provide stimulus and choice for the child. Appropriate instruments include a pair of 6-in cymbals, an 8-in flat drum, a pair of bongo drums, and a 3-ft standing drum. The small instruments are placed on the table, the large drum on the floor between the child and the therapist (the examiner). Objects that might distract the child are usually removed.

When the child enters the room, he is invited to sit on a chair facing the examiner. These chairs are placed close enough so the two may sit knee to knee, which helps the child focus attention on the task at hand. No training in music is required of either the examiner or the child. The ability to produce a rhythmic pattern on a simple percussion instrument and to observe carefully and record the behavior of the child is all that is required of the examiner. The child's task is to reproduce the examiner's rhythmic pattern.

Most children are attracted to the test materials and they will spontaneously choose from the several instruments offered. The children are curious and tend to explore and use the instruments placed before them promptly. If a child does not spontaneously choose an instrument, the examiner can offer the child his choice and when he chooses an instrument, invite him to tap a pattern. The unusual sounds, which can easily be produced on these instruments, are a source of pleasure to the child and maintain attention more readily than the dull sounds produced by tapping pencils on blocks in other tapping tests. The child's cooperation is also facilitated by the examiner's relaxed attitude. The test is therefore conducted in a pressure-free manner, with no specific time limit set for the production of the rhythmic pattern. All of these factors contribute to the success of the test.

If at the end of several tries, the child is unable to reproduce the examiner's rhythmic pattern on any one of the various percussion instruments available to him, the examiner terminates the session and suggests a return visit. What needs to be borne in mind is that, in this test, the ability to reproduce a tapping pattern is of the essence, not the length of time it takes to do so.

The term *rhythmic tonal pattern* refers to the distribution of long and short accented taps over a continuous fundamental beat. The following combinations are examples of variations of acceptable tapping patterns that can be presented to children. In this shorthand of sorts, a dash like this — stands for a tap of long duration, and a dot like this · represents a tap of short duration. These variations in taps are as follows:

1. —·—
2. —··—
3. —·—·—
4. ·—·—·—

Other variations are both possible and acceptable. The

object is to discern whether the child can reproduce rhythmic tapping that consists of a variety of specific patterns of long and short duration. It is advisable to begin with a short pattern such as found in example 1. If the child can reproduce this, the examiner proceeds to the next more complicated pattern. The examiner records the results of each attempt at the rhythmic patterns. An example of a variety of rhythmic patterns can be found by translating the familiar melodic pattern from "Battle Hymn of the Republic" into long and short taps. Two phrases from the song follow:

Glory, glory, Hallelujah

—·—·—·— —

Mine eyes have seen the glory of the

— —·—·—·—·

The examiner needs to wait and attend carefully for the child to produce a rhythmic pattern, because some children take time to stroke, shake, and generally explore the percussion instruments. If the child eventually produces such a pattern, the examiner enthusiastically imitates it a few times on one or another of the instruments. If it appears that the child does not produce a pattern, the examiner picks up an instrument and produces one. The percussive pattern and an encouraging nod from the examiner usually stimulates the child to try to repeat the pattern. Some children, however, even though they show interest in the stimulus pattern, fail to imitate the examiner. In such instances, the examiner either repeats the rhythmic tapping on the same instrument or taps out the same pattern on a different sounding instrument, which is then presented to the child with an invitation to repeat the pattern. To ensure accuracy of observation, the child is encouraged to reproduce the pattern on several instruments.

If the child can repeat the examiner's rhythmic tonal pattern, it can be assumed that the child is able to process and reproduce sound effectively. Only if he can do this is the next step taken. This further step determines whether the child can reproduce the pattern with auditory cues but without visual ones. The procedure is as follows: the examiner stands behind the child so that he does not merely imitate just what he sees and tells the child, "Now, I'm going to stand behind you and tap a pattern. Don't tap it until I say go, so that you will be sure to hear all of it." Children are usually eager to be involved in this pleasurable challenge and participate enthusiastically. The examiner begins by tapping the simple rhythmic pattern in the same manner as before and waits for the child's response. New information about the child may emerge. A child who successfully reproduced a pattern when visual cues were available may not be able to do so when relying solely on auditory cues. The implications for teaching approaches for such a child are significant as he will need visual cues to accompany auditory information.

Some children, as already indicated, never go beyond random tapping or thumping. These children should not be given any further testing that day but, as stated earlier, may be invited to come back another day for a second attempt. However, if a child continues to tap randomly rather than accurately reproduce the examiner's tonal rhythmic pattern, it is likely that the child suffers from neurological damage.

Results of a Preliminary Study

Over a period beginning in 1964, the Auditory–Motor Percussion Test was administered to a total of 347 children, ages 3–15. The research was conducted in neurological and psychiatric institutions, in a school for retarded and disturbed children, in a therapeutic nursery, and in a nursery and elementary school for presumably normal children.

Preliminary data showed most of the presumably normal 4 year old and older children passed the test. No tapping discrimination was evident in children younger than 4

years; that is, no 3 year olds passed the test. When the records available on the children who failed the test were
studied, evidence of neurological damage emerged in most
cases. In some cases, there was a history of anoxia at birth,
encephalitis, or a severe accident. Only a few of the children
who had failed were free of report of neurological damages.
It should be noted that some of the emotionally disturbed
children, including those who were autistic, were able to reproduce a rhythmic tonal pattern.

Controlled Study

On the basis of these suggestive findings, a more sys-
tematic, rigorous study contrasting normal and disturbed
children was undertaken from 1969 to 1971. The hypothesis
of this controlled study developed from the previous inci-
dental findings. The test results further demonstrated that
any child older than 4 years who was unable to reproduce a
rhythmic pattern is probably suffering from a dysfunction
of the central nervous system.

Many of the same settings used in the preliminary
studies were used for selection of 144 children as a norming
group for testing on the basis of availability and age. The pi-
lot study suggested that children between the ages of 4 and
7 years provided an adequate range for testing purposes;
children below 4 years old could not perform the rhythmic
tapping test successfully; of those above 7 years, most could
perform it accurately. Therefore, a base age of 4 years and a
ceiling of 7 years were stipulated as the age range for the
Auditory–Motor Percussion Test in the research design. This
new group of 144 children was drawn from the normal population and was free of known deficit; they were identified
by the nursery or elementary schools they attended as children without known physical or psychological handicaps. A
comparison group of 84 children was drawn from settings

for the emotionally disturbed. Since no 4 year olds were available in these special institutions and schools, the age range of those tested from those settings extended from 5 to 7 years. This data is found in Table 1.

After the children were tested, classification was made according to their ability to produce the required rhythmic tonal pattern on a percussion instrument. Those who were able to pattern in the manner described above were classified as patterners. Those who could not pattern were classified as nonpatterners. Subsequently, an investigation of their records was made for possible evidence of central nervous system dysfunction.

As shown in Table 1, seven of the 144 children (4.9%) tested in settings for normal children were unable to produce a rhythmic pattern. When the medical records of this suspect population were further investigated, it was found

Table 1. Number and Percentage of Children Tested
in Settings for Normal and Disturbed
by Categories of Patterners and Nonpatterners

	N	Age (years)	With documented damage				Without damage			
			Nonpatterners		Patterners		Nonpatterners		Patterners	
			N	%	N	%	N	%	N	%
			Settings for Normal Children							
	74	5	6	8.1	0	0	0	0	68	91.9
	44	6	0	0	3	6.8	0	0	41	93.2
	26	7	1	3.8	2	7.7	0	0	23	88.5
Total	144		7	4.9	5	3.5	0	0	132	91.6
			Settings for Disturbed Children							
	56	5	30	53.6	0	0	0	0	26	46.4
	16	6	7	43.8	1	6.2	0	0	8	50.0
	12	7	10	83.4	1	8.3	0	0	1	8.3
Total	84		47	55.9	2	2.4	0	0	35	41.7

that all seven of these children suffered from central nervous system dysfunction caused by either automobile accidents or such conditions as encephalitis or rubella. Their teachers were then consulted. During interviews they mentioned that these children exhibited behavioral difficulties that interfered with their academic performance and functioning in class. The teachers observed that these children were hyperactive, awkward, had short attention spans, and speech or reading difficulties. None of the teachers had been aware of the documentation of the children's neurological damage. They merely described the children's behavioral deficits and learning inadequacies after it was discovered that the children were unable to reproduce the rhythmic tapping.

Had this neurological damage been revealed earlier, these children could have been provided with appropriate teaching techniques. Children such as these, who are unable to "take in" sound and then reproduce it, require sensorimotor approaches that enable them to learn through their most intact modalities.

As also shown in Table 1, 47 of the 84 children (55.9%) from settings for the disturbed were unable to reproduce a rhythmic tonal pattern. Documented neurological information about these nonpatterners was then sought. The records of the children who resided in or had attended neurological or psychiatric institutions were examined for specific information that had been noted in each record by the examining neurologist attached to the institutions from which the children were selected. Documented neurological information on the children from other settings was obtained and records were perused for the needed neurological information. When information was inadequate, with help of the school or parents, information was forwarded by the child's physician.

All 47 nonpatterning childen had a history of documented neurological damage. Of the 84 children referred from settings for disturbed children, only 49 were shown to have documented neurological damage. Of these 49 children, 47 were unable to reproduce the rhythmic tapping.

As previously noted in this chapter, many researchers have stated the difficulty of distinguishing children with emotional and neurological damage because of the similarity of such symptoms such as hyperactivity, impulsivity, and concentration impairment. As can be seen from the results of the current study, the Auditory–Motor Percussion Test accurately identified these 47 children as having neurological impairment by their inability to reproduce rhythmic patterns.

Although all 47 children were reported to have hard signs of central nervous system damage, the signs varied, and some children had several signs. The neurologists reported such hard signs as deviation of uvula, paralysis, nystagmus, and abnormal reflexes, such as Babinski. It should be noted that among the 84 children, there were two with documented damage who successfully produced the required rhythmic pattern. This would indicate that neurological damage does not absolutely preclude ability to produce a rhythmic tonal pattern. Rather, and significantly, the presence of a structural alteration in the central nervous system is probable if the child is unable to tap a rhythmic pattern as indicated above.

A separate group of 69 4-year-old presumably normal children became available for testing after the foregoing study and were given the Auditory–Motor Percussion Test. The responses of these children from normal settings are of interest: of the 69 tested, 55 or 79% could pattern. The remaining 14 nonpatterners fell into two groups. In one group there were two children with documented central nervous system dysfunction; in the other, 12 children were without documented dysfunction. However, teachers did mention that some of these children were awkward or slow. It is these 4 year olds for whom the Auditory–Motor Percussion Test is especially significant. Their inability to reproduce the rhythmic tonal patterns can alert teachers and mental health professionals "early on" in their school experience to these significant hidden deficits and, as a result, help them prevent further academic and emotional lag in these children.

Summary

It is imperative that children with neurological damage be promptly and accurately identified so that they can achieve their optimum development. Once the neurological impairment is identified, appropriate, specific teaching approaches can begin. By failing to understand the true obstacle to learning in children with neurological impairment who have been referred to settings for the disturbed, therapists often miss opportunities to help children.

What is significant about the Auditory–Motor Percussion Test is that the presence of a structural alteration in the central nervous system is probable if children 4 years and older are unable to tap a rhythmic pattern as heretofore described. This information is valuable and important to the therapist, whose task it is to help children in cognitive and behavioral development. The therapist may then adapt the teaching approach to the child's individual needs as revealed by the Auditory–Motor Percussion Test. When a structural deficit in the central nervous system is uncovered, the therapist should use the sensorimotor approach to learning described in Chapter 6.

When this information on central nervous system deficit is unavailable, children who are capable of learning adequately fail to do so. Thus these children are unfortunately and repeatedly cast into a failure mold. Year after year they are dubbed with such damning terms and generalities as "withdrawn," "hyperactive," "awkward," "having short attention span," or "having speech or reading difficulties." The self-esteem of these children is lowered, and they do not master what they are capable of learning. Often they are intellectually and emotionally crippled for a lifetime and known only as having behavior problems.

It is apparent from the research that the Auditory–Motor Percussion Test reveals hidden neurological damage in children whose deficits might otherwise remain undiscovered. The test is especially valuable for use with anxious, "at-risk" children in school and in clinical situations because of the ease, practicality, and effectiveness with which it can be utilized by both child and examiner.

II

Specific Referral Difficulties and the Paraverbal Communication Response

5

The Abused Child

Case 1—H

Initial Sessions

H was a handsome 4-year-old boy who was referred for Para-verbal assessment and treatment. On interviewing the parents, both professional people, they described him as an insufferable disruptive, hyperactive child. They said the only solution to obtain the peace at home that they required at the end of an exacting working day was to do one of two things: If he annoyed them at the table, to tie him to his chair and "paddywhack" him, or, if they were in the living room having drinks and he annoyed them, to "paddywhack" him and then lock him in the closet.

The following are excerpts from several Paraverbal Communication sessions. These excerpts of the Paraverbal strate-

gies used will be followed by explanatory comments as to
the purpose of each maneuver used.

On entering the therapy room, H looked with interest at
the colorful array of materials on the table: clay, finger paint,
and percussion and string instruments. He appeared extremely fearful, merely looking but not touching anything.
The therapist then rhythmically strummed the autoharp.
These sounds could not be shut out. In spite of his anxiety,
he was participating, however minimally, in the session. He
attended but looked anxious and began to flap his hands.
The therapist stopped strumming and immediately changed
to a less stimulating kind of material. She placed some clay
in front of him. He fingered it gently and was intrigued.
First he pulled it, then squeezed it, and then pounded it
over and over. Not once did he look up at her. She participated with him by improvising to the tune of "Frère Jacques," a chant about what he was doing. It went, "H is
pulling, H is pulling, H is squeezing, H is pounding the
clay. I like his clay play, yes I do, yes I do." He looked surprised and smiled as he looked up at her. Then she took a
tiny cymbal and started cutting the clay in small pieces with
its edge. He was intrigued and happily took the cymbal and
copied her cutting movements over and over again. After a
while, he lost interest and, without preamble, he walked
over to a large paper basket and jumped in. "Cover me!" he
said. The therapist did. Then, from under the cover, he
shouted gleefully, "Find me, find me." The therapist pretended not to know where he was, looked all around, and
chanted gleefully, "Where, oh where is H?" It was their
"first conversation." He was ecstatic as an infant playing
peek-a-boo when she lifted the cover from the paper basket
and shouted, "There he is!" Then, from the paper basket
hiding, he spontaneously hid behind chairs and under ta-
bles, shouting, "Find me, find me!" This ignored, battered
little boy was surprised and in ecstasy that the therapist
found him. The next maneuver was catching soap bubbles
that the therapist blew toward him as she chanted, "Catch

them, smash them. H is smashing bubbles, yes he is." He loved their reciprocal involvement, the therapist blowing bubbles and H catching and smashing them, as she described in lyrics what he was doing. When this maneuver was over, he didn't want to leave. He had experienced such pleasure.

At the next two sessions, H insisted on going through the same maneuvers that they had previously done, with many variations. Gone was the withdrawn and anxious look. Good eye contact and childish pleasure were exhibited instead.

As the therapist observed his changing behavior, she wondered when they would uncover who or what was at the root of his problem. To pursue this goal, after a few moments had passed, the therapist interrupted the sequence of maneuvers and tried introducing a new maneuver, finger painting. Nearby were some puppets. H looked at the puppets, then at the messy paints in the various cups, with curiosity and anxiety. How could he dare to touch anything like the sticky finger paints he saw before him? To encourage him, the therapist grabbed a glob of paint and threw it at the nearby easel, whereupon the paint fell to the floor. She shouted, "Grab it, pick it up!" He leaned over, grabbed the paint from the floor, and then looked horrified at his paint-laden hands. "Wipe it on the paper," the therapist said, pointing to the paper on the easel. He was terrified at the sight of his messy hands. He seemed unable to move, so the therapist picked up some finger paint and made her own handprint on the paper. He was enchanted. The therapist said again, "Wipe your hand on the paper." He did, as he saw her do and saw his own finger prints. Again, he looked at his hands and became frightened. "Wash it! Wash it!" he gasped. The therapist turned the faucet on full force, laughed mischievously and said, "Wow! Here we go." He got caught up in the excitement of the rushing water and her jubilance. He then leaned over and turned on both faucets in a kind of game. Suddenly, he stopped and said, "Must not waste water, get fined." The therapist laughed and said, "That's in Jersey where you live. Here it's okay." Once more, he leaned over to the faucet and resumed his water orgy, while she encouraged and supported him by chanting, "More, more!" At the same time, the therapist tapped loudly on the drum to intensify her approval and support of what he was doing. Meanwhile the water was getting colored blue from all the blue finger paint on his hand.

Suddenly he stopped, leaned over to the table near the sink where all the materials were, picked up a male puppet, and smudged its face with blue finger painting. Then he threw it in the water, filled with sink with even more water, and said, "There he goes. We don't have to see *him* any more." The therapist asked, "Who?" He said, "Daddy." The therapist continued, "Now let's put black paint in the sink and we won't be able to see him at all." He did what she said, then turned to her and very seriously said, "Say a bad word." The therapist said, "No, you say a bad word." He said, "No, you say it." She hesitated because the family from which he came was a formal, reserved Catholic family. Then, she reconsidered, and thought that since they regularly go to church, they must all hear the word frequently, so she gratified him and yelled, "Hell." He looked merry, laughed, and said, "Damn it!" which the therapist repeated and said, "Hell, damn it!" He rapidly went on with a string of curse words, which behavior the therapist repeated. H wound up yelling, "Jesus Christ, you asshole jerk!"

When he got to the last word, looking at the therapist with a face filled with wild fury, she finally asked, "When does Daddy say these things to you?" He immediately became sober and pale and whispered, "When I can't stop running around and flapping my hands and jabbering. Then he ties me to my chair and paddywhacks me!" Tears came in his eyes. The therapist put her arm around him and said softly, "That's sad." Then she tenderly wiped his eyes and gave him the towel on which to dry his hands. She patted him on the shoulder to comfort him and to let him know that she understood. After the strain of releasing so much fear and hidden anger, even though much of it was done metaphorically, the therapist then said, "Let's go upstairs to Mommy" (the therapy room was on a lower floor). He had communicated enough for one day.

To the therapist's surprise, his mother was standing agitated at the top of the stairs that led to the therapy room. She had been eavesdropping. When she saw us she said, "You know, we don't usually use such language in our home. It's just when he gets so restless that we can't stand another minute of it that we just have to let go and let him have it." She looked at the therapist distraught, ashamed, and pleading with her. The therapist said, "I understand. Perhaps we should meet before H's next session and talk things over." She agreed. They made a date and for the first time both parents openly talked about their rage over H's behavior and their need to do something about it. During this session, both parents revealed abusive episodes in their own childhoods. The therapist discussed the problem with them and made suggestions as to how to ease the tension and anger they all felt. They were eager to cooperate.

Behavior on the part of H and his parents gradually improved. At his mother's suggestion, H's teacher came all the way from New Jersey, where he lived and taught school, to see the therapist too. His teacher reported that H's behavior had improved at school and he had begun to play with other children in school. His parents reported a similar improvement at home. Communication between parents, child, and the therapist developed to the point that it was satisfactory for all concerned.

Comments

The first maneuver, the strumming of an autoharp, was used to capture H's attention with its novel sound, since he was such a withdrawn child. Although the novel sound did succeed in capturing his attention, his anxiety was so great that the engaging sound seemed to distress him. He started flapping his hands and looking up at the ceiling. This was a signal to the therapist to use a less intrusive maneuver with which to get him to communicate. She put a lump of clay before him on the table. This was easier for him to cope with. He could use it, pull it, and squeeze it, without its having to become a specific correct and accurate object like a figure or a vase. The descriptive lyrics the therapist improvised saying how much she liked his clay work provided him with the approval he was so sorely lacking at home. The lyrics that say, "H is having fun" are not only part of a structured rhythm but are, with their rhyme, a source of pleasure. She joined him, and their synchronous work in cutting the clay with the edge of the tiny cymbal provided him with several therapeutic experiences. It gave him an opportunity to discharge tension from his anxiety and hidden anger, together with more of the much needed support and approval of an empathic adult. This support and approval of his behavior are basic needs for an abused child like H, a child who was ignored or punished when he became active. Another supportive experience came from the specificity of the approving lyrics the therapist improvised. His desperate need to be recognized approvingly was satisfied through permission granted to him to be creative when he invented the game of having the therapist find him in the basket. The gratification of the need to be affirmatively recognized was reinforced by his discovery of numerous places to hide and be found, such as behind chairs, in closets, and so forth. The smashing of the soap bubbles was another opportunity to discharge hidden anger and tension. Once again, approval was provided by the therapist's improvising lyrics encouraging him to smash the bubbles that she blew. The reciprocal behavior between her blowing and his smashing the bubbles was still another reinforcement of the profoundly needed approval. It was no wonder he did not want to stop the maneuver.

The continuation of these strategies formed a base for his communicating about the specific abuse and rigid home life. This base for revelation was found in the rich and varied communication evoked by his use of the finger paint strategy. His terrified gasping of "Wash it, wash it" communicated vividly what happened at home when he dirtied himself as does any little boy his age.

After the breakthrough session, there were sixteen additional sessions with H as well as regular monthly sessions with both parents. In addition, the mother frequently asked to talk to the therapist after H's sessions, at which times H would play in the therapy room by himself. Occasionally there were emergency telephone calls when tension at home became overwhelming.

Case 2 — L

The First Session

On arrival at the first session, the therapist asked the mother to join her 6-year-old daughter, L, and the therapist. At first the mother refused. The abusive parent is usually not only reluctant to seek help but may actively avoid it. The therapist told her that she understood how she felt but that this situation was different. The therapist said, "What I'd appreciate is your point of view on how L uses the materials and what you think of the way she behaved in general. I need your help. After all, she is your child and you know her much better than I do." The mother agreed, and with this they began the first of their joint sessions.

L came in and glanced at the materials on the table but touched nothing. The therapist picked up a drum and tapped a little rhythmic pattern. L was intrigued as the therapist repeated it loudly, then softly. Next, the therapist put it back on the table. Without picking it up, L tapped it lightly. The therapist promptly imitated L. She was surprised and delighted, as was her mother, sitting nearby. The therapist encouraged L to tap it again, and soon they were tapping, alternately loud and soft, fast and slow. The mother got caught up in the rhythm, at first just tapping with her foot.

Then she accepted the tambourine that the therapist offered her. They tapped together and had a happy time. Following this the therapist had them stand up and introduced tiny cymbals for each one to tap, at first with rhythms like the ones they did on the drum. Then new rhythms were introduced. The use of the cymbals in a standing position provided an opportunity for a different kind of movement, as well as greater freedom. It also gave the therapist an opportunity to observe L in a different body movement. Next, they all took turns tapping against each other's cymbals with their own cymbals while the therapist improvised instructive chanting to the tune of "Frère Jacques": "I tap L, L taps me, I tap Mommy, Mommy taps me, L taps Mommy, Mommy taps L," and so forth. All this was done with the same alternately fast and slow, loud and soft techniques that they had used in the drum tapping. Both L and her mother were delighted. After these pleasurable experiences, it now seemed that L was ready to move from the neutral area of tapping to a problem area. The therapist therefore introduced metaphoric use of lyrics related to a problem L's parents had reported when they brought her to the hospital. The therapist improvised lyrics to the folk tune "Kumbaya." The content of the lyrics had to do with a child's eating in her parents' bed and making a mess—one of L's many asocial behaviors. The lyrics went, "Someone's eating in my bed, Kumbaya, someone's eating in my bed, Kumbaya," and so on.

It was easy for L and her mother to chant along with the therapist on the nonthreatening word, "Kumbaya." This pleasurable and stimulating "Kumbaya" experience quickly led to a spontaneous communication from L. She revealed with glee, "Sometimes I eat in Mommy's bed and make a mess!" Then she looked mischievously at her mother and her mother looked grim. Tension rose. To cope with this stress, the therapist quickly substituted a new and more neutral maneuver—rhythmic rope pulling. Without comment, she handed them a piece of rope and they quickly became absorbed in vigorous mutual rope pulling. With this maneuver, the therapist holds one end of the rope and the child holds the other. Meanwhile, the therapist chants descriptive instructions as follows: "I pull L, L pulls me." This is done with variation in tempo. When L and the therapist came to the end of the lyrics, the therapist handed her end of the rope to the mother, so that she and L each had an end to pull rhythmically to her chanting. While participating in this maneuver, the mother suddenly gave a violent yank on the rope, which threw L to the floor. L burst into tears. The therapist quickly sat down next to her, wiped her tears away, and put her arm around her shoulders. Her mother promptly sat down on the other side of her and gently gave her a hug as she had seen the therapist do. The therapist then took L's hand in her left hand and her mother's hand in her right hand. Without a word from the therapist, the mother leaned over and took L's free hand in her own hand. They formed a little circle. Then to the folk tune, "Did You Ever See a Lassie?" the therapist improvised and chanted the following intimate lyrics. "Here we are together, together, all sitting on the floor. We're rocking and singing together on the floor. We're touching and holding each other while we sit on the floor." This intimate nurturing strategy produced the appropriate moment for ending their session. L was sent outside to play with the other children on the ward. The mother stayed and spoke to the therapist about several matters. She began with the episode they had discussed, the one having to do with L's throwing up after eating in her parents' bed. This was followed by her perpetual rage against L and her many asocial behaviors and the varieties of severe punishments she administered, all to no avail. As she talked she was reminded of and began to tell of some of her own abused childhood. These confidences seemed to comfort her somewhat.

When it was time to go she turned to the therapist and said softly, "Don't call me Mrs. K., just call me Joan." The therapist smiled at her and said, "I'll be glad to." She left the room looking more at ease.

Comments

In this first session, the first maneuver, a rhythmic tapping pattern, made L feel acceptance and pleasure. The therapist's immediate acceptance of her choice of material, the drum, as well as the way she chose to use it, and for how long, were especially needed because of her parents' constant disapproval and punishment of her asocial behavior. The pleasure she felt as she tapped a rhythm and was imitated by the therapist came both from the unusual percussive sound of the drum and the satisfaction she felt in being imitated. This pleasure was intensified by her mother's joining them and the three of them enjoying themselves together. It was a step in the direction of compensating for the serious pleasure deficiency both mother and child had experienced throughout their respective abusive childhoods. The next maneuver, rhythmic cymbal tapping, was introduced to give the pleasure of a new sound, to provide variety of movements and to give the therapist an opportunity to further assess L's body movements. The novelty of the new sound of each instrument additionally reinforced L's pleasure, as well as the feeling of competence so sorely missing from her life as an abused child. Having the experience of doing a variety of pleasurable things was also nurturing for her.

With these nonthreatening maneuvers as a base, they could then move from a neutral area to a problem area, that is, L's eating in her parents' bed and making a mess. The introduction of the metaphoric use of lyrics describing this asocial behavior made it possible for communication about a sensitive subject to take place spontaneously. The joint chanting of the innocuous chorus word "Kumbaya" in the lyrics and the structure of the rhythm put L at ease. It became feasible for her to identify with the stimulating lyrics, "Someone's eating in bed, Kumbaya," and helped her to communicate her mischievous feelings in this asocial behavior. In turn, what L said stimulated a nonverbal angry communication from her mother in the form of a grim facial expression. All this developed into a feeling of extreme tension, which the therapist tried to reduce by introducing rhythmic rope pulling and chanting. However, this strategy backfired and elicited an unexpected response from her mother, who could no longer control her aggression. Abusing her child was too habitual; with one violent yank, she revealed her aggressive, abusive behavior toward her child as she pulled her to the floor.

The therapist was then challenged to convert this violence into a nonverbal nurturing situation, which also allowed the mother to observe the therapist as a model of appropriate behavior. The next maneuver, a quiet rhythmic circle, provided a pleasurable healing experience for both mother and child. Through mutual delight in the gentle rhythmic swaying and the comforting touch of each other's hands, all communicated nonverbally and there developed a beginning sense of trust. Then, the needed therapeutic relationship could be established. At this point, the child became able to discharge tension as well as ventilate ideas and feelings.

At the end of the Paraverbal Communication sessions, there was sufficient improvement in the parent–child relationship for L and her mother to be able to be transferred to traditional psychotherapy.

Summary

Paraverbal Communication, with its often metaphoric use of materials employed in the maneuvers, made feasible the achievement of the goals of the treatment of these two heretofore inaccessible child abuse cases. The Paraverbal rationale of acceptance and pleasure was of special usefulness in treating these rejected children, both of whom suffered not only physical abuse but also profound hidden emotional scars. In both cases, the deprivation of the parents in their youth made for immature unrealistic demands on their children. There was poor communication. Abusive behavior ensued. With the nurture from acceptance and pleasure

received, communication and increased maturity on the part
of all concerned developed. At the termination of both cases,
burgeoning appropriate behavior was manifest on the part
of both the adults and the children described.

6

Individual and Peer Learning

Paraverbal Communication
Empowers Children to Learn

Most children want to learn. But many lack the basic communication skills necessary to effectively understand and respond to the academic concepts presented to them in school. Research has indicated that cognitive and communication difficulties are prevalent among learning-disabled students (Wiig and Semel 1976). This is true whether the student's behavior is characterized by short attention span, hyperactivity, hypoactivity, lack of impulse control, or poor self-esteem. It has become increasingly clear that new ways must be found to develop communication skills in these children.

Pressure to find new ways to improve teaching effectiveness is building as increasing numbers of students are referred to special education classes because they cannot be taught in the regular classroom. During the 1985–1986 school year, over four million students, or 11% of the total public school enrollment, received services under the provision of the Education for Handicapped Children Act (PL94-142) (Gartner and Lipsky 1987). These students were placed in small classes and promised specially trained teachers using special materials designed to serve individual needs. However, there is currently very little innovation in teaching strategies or other adaptations for children with learning difficulties, and classrooms, despite their small size, remain "teacher centric" (Gartner and Lipsky 1987).

These students spend many school hours working on specific tasks involving math operations, phonics, vocabulary, spelling, decoding, and comprehension. However, improving communication skills is generally not on the daily agenda, even though this crucial factor often determines whether or not the student can learn the specific academic tasks mentioned.

The term *communication* in this chapter refers to giving and receiving information. In school, this means answering questions orally and in written form, listening to information presented, and reading. For most children to communicate effectively, they must (1) be in a nonthreatening environment and (2) have available a variety of ways to convey their thoughts and ideas. Children begin to learn effectively only when the messages that they receive make sense. Research and clinical observation indicate that learning-disabled students have great difficulty relying only on the word content in a learning situation. They need to be assisted by concrete experiences (Wiig and Semel 1976). The strategies presented in this chapter address this need and illustrate teaching methods utilizing each child's unique way of communicating and learning.

Paraverbal Communication is an effective method for remediating communication and language difficulties. Emphasis is on child-centered teaching strategies that turn experiences into understanding. This process builds self-confidence and promotes more effective communication and appropriate behavior. Paraverbal Communication strategies are all based on clear and ongoing two-way communication, respect for the child's autonomy, and trust.

Paraverbal Communication techniques give children concrete sensorimotor experiences so that they can acquire information. Since children can learn through many senses, including auditory, visual, kinesthetic, and tactile, teaching strategies utilizing a variety of sensorimotor experiences are often necessary. The techniques presented permit the therapist to adapt to each child's functioning, regardless of developmental level or diagnosis, in order to stimulate the desired learning and communication. There is significant opportunity for empowering children to learn, because the method can be tailored to the unique needs of each child.

Specifically, the child and the therapist participate in body movement and sound maneuvers often chosen by the child to communicate and interpret information. Maneuvers include initiating and imitating, dramatizing, and tapping rhythmic patterns and nonverbal rhythmic dialogues. Painting and working with clay and other materials are integrated into the maneuvers to achieve specific therapeutic goals. The underlying metaphoric technique for working with song lyrics enables children to appropriately ventilate feelings and discuss meanings of words and relevant issues through safe, familiar lyrics. Folk, popular, and improvised lyrics are used, depending upon what the child presents and the intervention that the therapist believes to be functional.

In addition to ventilating feelings, many language concepts, such as main idea, supporting details, characterization, and vocabulary, can be taught through the use of lyrics. For example, those found in the folk song "Nobody Knows the Trouble I've Seen" can be used to elicit the main idea, which is that a person has many troubles. Abstract thinking can be encouraged as well, as generalizations about lyrics are explored.

The child experiences power with his own body, and through sound, learns the meaning and emotion of words, which reading or hearing alone often does not provide. The child is responsive to learning because he can avail himself of a variety of pleasurable media through which communication can be established.

The following two examples illustrate how Paraverbal Communication techniques can be used to facilitate communication and teach language skills, first with a 9-year-old boy and then with a small group of 7-year-old children.

Individual Learning

K is a 9-year-old boy repeating the third grade, thought to be suffering unspecified neurological damage. He attends a class for students with learning disabilities for 1 hour each day. According to his regular classroom teacher, "you never know where K is...one day he'll partially attend to his work, another day he is unable to do simple class work. He's unpredictable. He has difficulties in all subjects."

The therapist began with the Auditory–Motor Percussion Test (Chapter 4), which has been found to suggest the presence of neurological damage through a child's inability to copy rhythmic patterns. According to the author of the test, children unable to copy patterns often have neurological damage. However, the ability to copy does not rule out the possibility of neurological damage. It is merely another indicator and should be used as such. Because of the sensorimotor approach, that is, the pleasurable rhythmic use of the body and the attractive percussion sound from drums, castanets, or other percussion instruments, this assessment does not feel like a test to children and therefore it is a good starting point and provides diagnostic information.

K was able to tap the simple rhythmic patterns correctly while watching the therapist and also when he had his back to her. He was able to remember, distinguish, and emphasize the appropriate number of taps, regular and syncopated. His ability to reproduce sounds suggested that he could learn by using materials that produced sound.

Percussion instruments are used in Paraverbal Communication because they attract attention through their unusual sound, are symbols of pleasure, and are simple to use so that a child quickly attains a sense of mastery, which is so basic to learning. In addition, percussion instruments stimulate appropriate discharge of the tension often common to the child with communication and learning difficulties.

Another key reason the student with learning difficulties is motivated by Paraverbal Communication is the offering of pleasurable choices—instruments, materials, and maneuvers, as well as how to use them. K was unable to make choices at first, but did so after the therapist chose an instrument. After seeing her choose, he was more comfortable making his own choice and began to experiment with the different materials. In each session, he began by choosing his favorite materials, making choices was no longer difficult for him since he was accepted, no matter what he chose. By being able to make choices, his self-image improved. He initiated patterns and movements, communicated his feelings, and chose songs and maneuvers.

K experienced much pleasure from his success with the rhythmic tapping and he was receptive to further learning through this maneuver. He and the therapist reinforced math operations through the rhythmic tapping. Depending upon the nature and severity of the learning difficulty, the therapist can introduce cognitive elements into the rhythmic tapping maneuver. "Let's tap 5 times, 6 times. Let's add 4 taps and 3 taps. Which hand did more taps? Let's tap it loud, now soft, fast, now slowly; with our nails, now our knuckles. How else can we tap it? Let's tap it with our feet. Let's clap it." Subtraction, multiplication, and division can also be learned and reinforced as both child and the therapist share the number tasks and actively solve them. While the child performs, he feels, hears, and sees the concepts of numbers and their operations. The learning possibilities are infinite as long as the child is pleasurably involved.

K experienced and learned the meaning of the words intensity, increase, and decrease by experiencing them. As the therapist directed soft to loud by moving her hands high for loud and low for soft, K followed her movement cues to increase and decrease his sound on the drum. They then reversed roles to enable K to direct the therapist and experience leading. By both following specific cues as well as creating them, he experienced and learned.

In the next session, K chose a large drum and he and the therapist began tapping syllables of words by categories. They took turns naming one-syllable words of animals (dog, cat, horse, cow) and simultaneously tapping the animal words. K suggested that they imitate the animal as they tapped and he showed the therapist how to do this by making a scratching motion on the drum for cat. In addition to giving auditory structure to the lesson, the percussion feature enabled K to experience the words through movement and helped him to recall names in sequence. Next, K suggested they think of two-syllable sports words (baseball, football, hockey), then two-syllable weather words (raining, snowing, sunny, windy). He became "invested" in the learning, because his ideas were accepted and incorporated. The rhythm provided the organizing component for remembering the number of syllables, and the pleasure and success K experienced by helping develop the strategy moved him ahead to higher levels of learning.

Rhythmic tapping is not an end in itself but leads to more complex maneuvers and learning, always at the child's own rate. The patterns that K initiated were successful because they were self-generated. The therapist was then able to build upon this positive feature and introduce tempo changes and other variations on different instruments, but still within the structure of K's original pattern. Through media diversity, he experienced many different sensations and sounds of his same pattern, while reinforcing the constant rhythmic identity. The transfer of learning about his own identity began to take place when he tapped his pattern on a drum, stamped it with his feet, snapped it with his fingers, and hit it with the cymbals using his arms. He discovered that this pattern remained intact regardless of how he created it. It was his pattern. The therapist reinforced K's unique movements as he created them, which clarified and strengthened his movements. What appears to be simple movement for many children may be the beginning of a sense of competency and identity for some children who have difficulty learning.

By using rhythmic tapping to demonstrate and integrate impulse control, the therapist and child can divide a pattern with the therapist tapping the first part and the child completing it. For example, ... — ... —. The child learns to wait for his turn and is motivated to wait and share because of the anticipated pleasure in doing his part. This maneuver helps him to distinguish his part or "the important part" auditorily, visually, and kinesthetically because it is "his" part. By incorporating his name into the maneuver and tapping it rhythmically on the instrument of his choice, slow, fast, soft, or loud, he learns about syllables, his self-esteem is raised by hearing his name repeated so many ways, his identity is reinforced, and he becomes more receptive to learning in general.

After the seated maneuver using the drum, the therapist believed that K would respond well to a maneuver in which he could stand and move his body. In this maneuver which involved role playing, he would have the opportunity to learn first by following and then by leading. The therapist selected the song "Whatever I Do, Do Like Me," stood up, and made a movement for K to copy. At first he appeared timid when asked to copy even simple movements. However, when the therapist copied even his involuntary gestures, he saw that his motions were recognized and accepted, and he then began to initiate specific movements for her to copy. This validation of a child's movement, whatever it is, rarely fails to get him to participate. As K became more confident that his movements were accepted by the therapist's imitation, his movements became more animated and differentiated from hers. In addition to helping raise a child's self-esteem and teaching impulse control by having him wait his turn, this maneuver can permit the therapist to incorporate many cognitive motor experiences and build vocabulary. A word can be dramatized and defined through movement. Within the structure of the song, "Whatever I Do, Do Like Me," the child can also appropriately ventilate aggressive feelings by punching and stamping dramatizations. The maneuver reinforces for the child in many dramatic ways, the capabilities of his body.

After a maneuver involving body movement while standing children usually need and welcome the control involved in a seated maneuver. By introducing maneuvers according to the observed needs of the child, the therapist strengthens their relationship and sustains the child's high interest. They can use the autoharp to reestablish a sense of connectedness as part of the harp is placed on the child's lap and part on the therapist's lap. Children enjoy identifying family members and themselves by plucking appropriate sounding strings of the autoharp. K plucked a low sound for Father, medium for Mother, and a high but soft sound for himself. He was delighted with his sound characterizations of his family and the pleasure the autoharp provided. In this maneuver, the therapist can observe how and where the child sees himself in the family constellation. Small muscle coordination can also be observed. A child can accompany a therapist's songs or improvised lyrics related to his learning or emotional difficulty. After experiencing the pleasure of producing the music sound and hearing important words emphasized, the child is usually eager to talk about the interesting story lyrics. This metaphoric use of lyrics permits children to talk about problems in a nonthreatening way and learn language concepts too. The main idea of the song can be discussed objectively and the song lyrics can be related to others' problems first and then function as a bridge to the child's own difficulties.

For example, K communicated in many ways that he

wanted his father to be more involved with him. He had stated through other maneuvers that his father was "always busy in the basement" and didn't have time for him. The therapist chose the song "Take Me Out to the Ballgame" in order for K to have pleasure with the content of the song and the success of accompanying her on the autoharp. As the autoharp was placed on his lap and bridged to the therapist's, a connectedness was established and K felt safe to improvise lyrics with her. They sang the first verse together. Afterward, the therapist sang, "Take me out to the ____" and asked K to tell her where else they could go. He responded and they continued until the therapist felt it was safe to add, "Dad and I go out to the ballgame." K smiled and joined her in singing the new lyrics. They then added K's suggestions of other places to go with his father. K showed great pleasure in the thought of such involvement with his father and the therapist obtained ideas about K's preferred places to go with his father. The therapist could then, at the appropriate time, talk to K's father about his wishes or include the parents in one of their sessions so that they could participate with their son and learn how to communicate more effectively with him.

The song, "Honey, You Can't Love One," enabled K to supply words that rhyme with the therapist's words,

> you can't love one and still have __ fun
> two __ true...three __ free...four __ more

The song led to discussion of many feelings, such as love, jealousy, freedom, and so on. The repetition and predictability of the melody and lyrics liberated K to continue through 5, 6, and 7, and rhyme the numbers, thereby building language and freeing him to ventilate feelings about the words he selected. A child with learning problems often needs to recognize his own as well as others' feelings. To further this goal and to provide continuing interest, the therapist can introduce a new instrument. She handed K the large cymbals and told him to choose among four kinds of feelings (happy, sad, angry, and scared) and to dramatize a feeling using the cymbals. The therapist told him to show the feeling on his face, and she would try to guess his feeling. The child can be asked to show the opposite feeling from the one he just showed or a similar feeling, thereby building additional vocabulary. The therapist and the child then reverse roles to enable the child to guess the therapist's feeling and be the one "in control." Many language arts skills can be conceptualized through the use of materials and then expanded through verbal teaching.

Since pleasure for the child and a feeling of competence are always elements present in Paraverbal Communication, structured maneuvers that meet the child's needs and materials that especially appeal to the child are presented. By offering a nerf ball, which is familiar and pleasurable to a child, the therapist can make suggestions which help him to pace his movements and reinforce academic concepts. K tossed the ball high into the air, clapped, and counted as he caught it. He then tossed it higher and counted by twos, "2, 4, 6" before catching it. More complex arithmetic such as addition or multiplication can be built into the maneuver and children are generally eager to suggest and decide what to learn next. Syllables, specific categories, and many other concepts can be incorporated into this maneuver, which provides pleasure, rhythmic structure, and an appropriate learning challenge.

Another standing movement maneuver that provides additional diagnostic value is chalking to evocative music. This maneuver engages the child visually, auditorily, and kinesthetically and provides another means of release of tension. The chalking involves only responsive chalk strokes, not objective drawing where a child might feel he can make a mistake. Because of the subjectivity of the maneuver, the child's self-esteem is raised because his chalking cannot be wrong. It is the process that is important—the involvement of a child rather than the product.

The therapist encourages the child to listen to the music before beginning to chalk on large poster paper clipped to an easel. She can point out or ask the child to note the various sounds in the music (loud, soft, fast, slow, big, tiny, running sounds, walking sounds, sad, happy, strong sounds, and so on) and suggest he move his body and make chalk strokes in response to what he hears. After a child has chalked a few times and becomes accustomed to the maneuver, he usually begins to use his body much more freely, often tapping his feet as he chalks and choosing many colors to communicate his feelings. This freer use of the body is the desired goal in order for the child to experience his power and freely communicate what he feels. After chalking, the child enjoys telling the therapist about his product. From the child's choice of colors, intensity of the chalk pressure, and the overall production, the therapist can often learn the child's hidden thoughts and feelings.

The therapist can also join the child in the chalking maneuver on the other side of the easel. In this way, the child sees the therapist taking pleasure in producing her personal chalking creation. Afterward, discussion can take many forms. Each participant can describe the feelings evoked by the music, how the colors and chalk strokes show these feelings. They can talk about the unique differences and similarities in the child's and the therapist's products.

After a Paraverbal Communication session, children usually ask to return. They are motivated to return because of the pleasure, the stimulating age-appropriate use of the maneuvers, and the resultant sense of competence they have thereby achieved. Their ongoing success encourages them to attempt new maneuvers and to risk new experiences. Paraverbal Communication encourages, stimulates, and expands children's resource capabilities. Their resultant increased confidence is an outcome of success, acceptance, and pleasure and paves the way for new challenges. Children who have had difficulty learning in ways not compatible with their specific needs find their own unique ways of learning inspired through Paraverbal Communication. They begin to experience a new definition of self in a context that ensures success.

Learning among Peers through Paraverbal Communication

The power of peer influence has been widely documented in the literature. Children learn from each other in a group when they are provided with conditions and opportunities to interact in constructive ways, gain their peers' acceptance, and communicate. Paraverbal Communication is a powerful teaching and socializing concept for groups because it embodies specific, unique sound and movement maneuvers tailored to children in a group. Because Paraverbal maneuvers permit nonverbal communication through the use of many pleasurable sensorimotor experiences, children with varied learning styles and behavior are motivated to participate and cooperate. Children can interact in two ways: individually or as a group. Verbal interaction is often individual. However, the manner of using the materials in Paraverbal Communication permits group interaction because of the very nature of the sensorimotor approach. For example, tapping percussion instruments, creating body movement, and chanting lyrics all are enhanced and intensified by group action.

Children welcome the regular opportunites to make choices from the percussion instruments and other novel Paraverbal materials. They are empowered by the flexibility of using the materials in ways that highlight their contributions. The appealing concrete communicative tools gain and maintain the attention of the children and stimulate them to take the initiative in many learning situations and to cooperate with peers. This kind of pleasurable, constructive participation results in less need for children to seek attention through unsocialized, controlling behavior.

The potential benefits to children learning together through Paraverbal Communication in a group include gains in actual learning, increased sensitivity to others' feelings, a reduction in passivity and/or aggression, increased self-esteem, and a new ability to communicate.

In the session that follows, three children were selected

because they were unable to learn in larger classes. One child's aggressive behavior interfered with his learning and the other two children were extremely withdrawn and unable to participate in class. The therapist accepted these differences but structured the aggressive and withdrawn behavior with flexible Paraverbal maneuvers to teach and modify the behavior of all three children.

To establish intimacy and be able to control the children, the therapist should sit close to the three children. The aggressive child should be placed between the two withdrawn children and thus the withdrawn children are usually stimulated and encouraged to participate as they observe the pleasure of their active, aggressive neighbor. The therapist sits opposite the children and has at his side a variety of percussion and simple string instruments that attract and command the children's attention: bongos, tambourine, hand drum, floor drum, castanets, autoharp, and/or guitar. The enthusiastic and accepting manner of the therapist contributes to the children's willingness to learn.

Illustrative Technique 1: Teaching Word Opposites

To help decrease anxiety and to promote an atmosphere of acceptance, the children are given the privilege of choosing whichever instrument they would like to tap. The therapist then taps and chants the rhythmic pattern of the name belonging to the first child, for example, *Jenn*-ifer. All three children are encouraged to join the therapist in tapping and chanting the first child's name, repeating it four times in succession—first slow, then fast; loud, then soft. This usually produces constructive behavioral results. First, the child whose name is used is pleased at being the focus of activity and attention. It often is a first step toward raising the self-image and decreasing anxiety. The same procedure is followed for the names of the other two children, who want to share in the pleasure (Ginnot 1961). They quickly learn the necessity of waiting their turn so that their own names can then be the center of attention. With this strategy, impulse control often begins to improve. Also, the pleasurable, stimulating repetition involved can be a beginning of extended attention span (Heimlich 1972) and reinforces memory when learning more complex tasks. Moreover, the structure inherent in this rhythmic percussive work is of special help in organizing random movements, particularly those of the hyperactive child (Gardner 1974, Fields 1954).

These burgeoning affirmative behavioral changes form a basis for the therapist to move on to the next step in her objectives: helping the children achieve cognitive goals like the learning of word opposites such as those found in the concept of slow and fast. Even in this more demanding learning situation, the therapist is able to continue the basic use of pleasure, acceptance, and repetition because of the variety of sensorimotor tools for communication available in the Paraverbal Method. Then she can institute a new body position, for example standing (Gerhardt 1973), and the children are encouraged to use slow and fast in rhythmic clapping, shoulder shaking, foot tapping, and hip swaying to help them further concretely experience the concepts of slow and fast (Ginsburg and Opper 1969). While they perform, they feel, hear, and see the concept they are supposed to learn.

Illustrative Technique 2: Teaching Phonemes

The setting is the same as in technique 1. The cognitive goal of learning phonemes can be approached through using the tune of a familiar nursery song like *Mary Had a Little Lamb* and substituting the phonemes to be learned for the words of the original song:

Original words:
Mar y had a lit tle lamb
Substitute phonemes:
Mad mad mad mad mad mad mad

At this point the therapist inserts the connecting phrase

"rhymes with" so that she can introduce additional phonemes. This sequence continues as follows:

Original words:
Lit tle lamb Lit tle lamb
Substitute phonemes:
Sad sad sad Bad bad bad

The substitute phonemes are sung until the end of the tune is reached. The same basic techniques as were used early in the session for name syllable tapping are now applied to reinforce the phoneme work, that is, accompanying rhythmic clapping, stamping, and so on, in various tempos. The learning can be expanded by repeating the word, for example mad, and dramatizing the evoked feelings by hitting the drum. After this, the therapist can ask the children to name other words that have similar meanings such as angry and upset. In addition to expanding vocabulary, this new emotional dimension strengthens the meaning of the words for the children and provides for release of tension as well.

Illustrative Technique 3: Teaching Sequencing

A variation of technique 2 is used by having the therapist and children sing the sequence of the days of the week to the familiar tune of the chorus of the "Battle Hymn of the Republic" thus:

Original words:
Glo ry Glo ry Hal le lu jah
Substitute words:
Mon day Tues day Wednes day Thurs day

The therapist continues to sing to the end of the chorus and thus is able to fit in and repeat the sequence of the seven days of the week (Heimlich 1972). Many other word sequences such as seasons or months of the year can be learned through this strategy that reinforces concepts through pleasureful repetition.

Illustrative Technique 4: Teaching Homonyms

In this cognitive experience, the lyrics of popular folk songs are used as a channel for communication and learning. For example, if the word *lies* is to be taught as a homonym, two folk songs can be introduced. In each song, *lies* is set in a totally different context that clearly illustrates how the same word can have different meanings in different settings. For example, the therapist can use a verse from the old folk song "My Bonnie Lies over the Ocean" to teach the homonym *lies*, as follows:

> My Bonnie *lies* over the ocean
> My Bonnie *lies* over the sea
> My Bonnie *lies* over the ocean
> Oh, bring back my Bonnie to me

This can be followed by the old Kentucky mountain song *On Top of Old Smoky*, the fourth verse of which goes like this:

> She'll hug you and kiss you
> And tell you more *lies*
> Then the cross ties on the railroad
> Or stars in the skies

Each song should be sung with feeling by the therapist and children with accent on the homonym *lies*. After each song is sung, the meaning of the verse in general and then the central meaning of the homonym to be learned should be discussed. Dramatization can be added to this technique (Gerhardt 1973). With the tension release experienced by body movement and pleasurable singing, the therapist establishes a bridge that leads to readiness for the discussion of the different affective meanings to be found in the homonym *lies*. The foregoing strategy often releases spontaneous discussion rooted either in other folk songs or in real life situations. The result frequently is a further contribution to language development.

Illustrative Technique 5: Development of Hand–Eye Coordination

Each child stands before an easel to which there is clipped 12 × 16-in. black drawing paper. A box of 1-in. pastel chalk is on a chair at each child's side and a recording is ready to be played. A march or other markedly rhythmic composition is used as a stimulus for the chalking. The children are told to close their eyes briefly and move their hands in the air while keeping time to the music as soon as it begins. After they have listened and moved for about a minute, they are told to open their eyes and to take some chalk, one piece in each hand and to chalk on the paper in a random pattern that develops in rhythmic response to the music.

This technique helps in the development of hand–eye coordination. There is keen, sensuous pleasure from the combination of the rhythmic use of colored chalk and moving hands, feet, and head to music. There is satisfaction, too, in the sight of unexpected designs that the music and chalk strokes evoke. The fact that no limits are placed on the manner in which the children chalk and that each individual can create a unique, accepted product seems to give deep satisfaction. For the child whose pervasive feeling is that he has nothing within him that is of value, this experience contribues to raised self-esteem.

As shown here, the therapists of children with learning difficulties can use their own creative inner resources in place of, or in addition to, standard methods of teaching and developing socialization skills in children. The Paraverbal Method lends itself to group work because the nonverbal maneuvers permit and encourage simultaneous participation. Paraverbal Communication makes achievement of goals possible for both children and those mental health professionals working with them.

7

The Mentally Retarded Child

Retarded Children Communicate
through the Paraverbal Approach

Professionals who work with exceptional children, whether they are of high or low intelligence need to meet the challenge of enabling them to communicate. Communication with retarded children is particularly challenging because these children have not reached age-appropriate development in many areas and therefore often cannot communicate adquately in either behavioral or cognitive situations.

Many retarded children are characterized by apathy, others by extreme excitability. Their inability to communicate produces anxiety and a poor self-image, which are additional roadblocks to optimum cognitive and behavioral

121

achievement. Many retarded children are restless, destructive, unable to concentrate or cooperate, aggressive, and tense; all these behaviors contribute to school difficulty or failure. They often have problems relating to each other, as well as to their teachers. Many are not only unable to function satisfactorily in the classroom and in the playground, but they are also unable to accept psychotherapy.

Paraverbal Communication is an especially effective method for working with retarded children. The children do not have to cope with verbal demands, which are often beyond their competence. This is so because of the mostly sensorimotor approach of Paraverbal Communication.

This chapter will discuss Paraverbal Communication techniques used in early childhood, latency, and adolescence. The sound and movement maneuvers described in Chapter 3 can readily be adapted to help retarded children communicate. Examples of retarded children communicating through Paraverbal Communication consistently illustrate the Paraverbal rationale of pleasure and acceptance.

Early Childhood

The first group had children 4 and 5 years old with I.Q.'s in the 40 to 50 range. These children were characterized by anxiety, poor attention, and inability to communicate or relate to each other or to the therapist. When some of these children were particularly inaccessible in the regular class, they were seen in a smaller group of three, usually two withdrawn children and one restless child. For added control, the restless child can be seated between the two withdrawn children, who are generally intrigued and stimulated by their more active peer. Focus with these children is on achieving communication through sound and movement, because of the children's limited ability to use language. The maneuvers are adapted to the limited capacities of the young retarded children involved. Sensory motor input is emphasized, always using the same Paraverbal rationale of acceptance and pleasure throughout the sessions.

The following is a description of a typical Paraverbal session with one particular group of 5-year-old children who attended a Westchester public school. The group consisted of a 5½-year-old girl who was very withdrawn and two restless boys, also 5½ years old. The children were difficult to test but suggested I.Q.'s were 50.

All three were anxious, had limited vocabulary, and poor speech. The immediate goals were to help these children communicate, raise their self-esteem, help them relate to each other and to the therapist, and enable them to participate in classroom activity. Of course, the eventual goal was to help these children achieve their optimum potential.

In Chapter 2, the important role of touch was stressed. With these three retarded youngsters, most of the Paraverbal maneuvers involved touch to enable them to experience affect as they participated in movements while chanting affective words to describe them. Touch also provided the children with cognitive cues, as in the following maneuver. The therapist and children might begin by holding hands in a circle while chanting a descriptive lyric such as, "Here we are together all holding hands." New words and movements to accompany them were improvised after "Here we are together" such as "touching our ankles" followed by "our shoulders, our necks, our faces, our eyes, our hair," and so forth. All these touching experiences not only gave the children a feeling of communication through touch, but, with their sound and movement, also helped them to experience and learn with each repetition the words for the various parts of their bodies. It also helped them relate to each other and to the therapist in the pleasurable, structured, rhythmic maneuver that they shared together. With their repeated motions, the children had opportunites to constructively discharge tension and to raise their self-images as they jointly moved and touched the indicated parts of their bodies while, at the same time, observing each other. There was no display of disruptiveness on the part of the restless children because they were involved in pleasurable movement. The apathetic child was pleasurably structured and stimulated into movement, attention, and communication through placement between the restless children. These children who were now paying attention and involved in the movement maneuvers, discharged their hyperactivity appropriately through group rhythmic movements and descriptive chanting. The entire maneuver was then repeated, but the second time it was done very softly to maintain the children's attention through the contrast. After this variation, loud chanting of the same words was begun, again, to provide still another experience within the context of the familiar lyrics "Here we are together." This change of dynamics enabled the children to experience the pleasure made possible through their own ability to chant softly and then loudly.

Another variation still using the familiar lyrics is changing the tempo, at first chanting slowly and then fast. All these variations in dynamics and tempo provided many constructive opportunities for the children to communicate. The variations helped command and extend the children's attention and permitted the much needed repetition that retarded children require before they can gain the sense of mastery that is sorely needed by them. With their acquired sense of mastery came raised self-esteem and an improved sense of identity, decreased anxiety, increased ability to relate to each other and to the therapist, and above all a beginning ability to communicate. All of this helped toward the desired goal of achieving their optimum potential.

A similar Paraverbal technique emphasizing touch reinforced the desired goal of enabling the children to communicate. This was achieved through the use of a variety of simple materials such as play dough, elastic rope, percussion instruments, and soap bubbles.

These sound and movement experiences or "maneuvers" can all be expanded by the imaginative therapist. They are primarily simple early childhood activities used in any standard nursery school. However, what makes them significant and useful for the therapist of retarded children is *not* the use of the materials themselves but the awareness of the therapist as to *how* the materials need to be used to achieve the specific goals. For example, a child needing to ventilate feelings can be offered large cymbals, a drum, or clay, depending on specific factors. If the child is aggressive, a small percussion instrument or clay might be offered to appropriately channel his communication. However, a timid child might be offered a large percussion instrument purposefully to stimulate appropriate and adequate ventilation. Both types of children experience needed safety through the appropriate medium for each one and can let another person know their feelings. What is important is that the sensorimotor materials be used to enable children to communicate affect appropriately. In other words, the goal is communication; the route is pleasure and acceptance, the rationale for Paraverbal Communication. To expand this rationale further, the therapist must uncritically accept any motion of the child's as long as he participates. The obvious pleasure of the therapist, both in the maneuver and in the child's participation, contributes to the chief goal, which is communication. The attachment of pleasure to every maneuver leads not only to communication but to the desired end of optimum development, both cognitive and behavioral.

With the opportunity to utilize the sensorimotor sound and movement maneuvers, the children can easily take in, select, and connect information from the world around them. This learning all happens spontaneously. The children don't have to think about what they are learning because they are experiencing it. These varied experiences are repeated again and again, sometimes at different sessions and with different materials as they pleasurably develop the children.

Sometimes pleasurable variety is given to the Paraverbal techniques by changing the children's seating positions; for example, moving from the floor to a chair. Descriptive words that have to do with affect can be introduced and combined with motion. Instead of the emphasis on learning body parts, the therapist and children can chant, for example, "Here we are together all laughing, or crying, or all sad, or all angry, or all happy." Touch continues to play an important role in this maneuver as all in the group hold hands and are structured by the rhythm. Variety and a new body position is also introduced with the same melody using new active words, "Here we are together all standing on the floor, jumping, stamping, hopping, bending, stretching." The skillful therapist can convert her vast knowledge of childhood lyrics and materials into an endless variety of interactions in the service of communication. It must be emphasized that the acquisition of a list of cognitive achievements is definitely not the goal; rather, the goal is communication that leads to the appropriate desired cognitive and behavioral development.

Latency

This section of the chapter is devoted to illustrations of interactions with retarded children who are in the latency period. Among these children, the diminution of anxiety was basic to their ability to communicate. The setting for this work was a prominent facility for retarded youth. This residential institution houses boys and girls aged 8 to 18. They are all mentally retarded, many with emotional problems. These children attend a special public elementary school where classes may have as few as five pupils. Some adolescent children attend local vocational junior and senior high schools as a part of their movement back into the community. The facility's own reading, speech, and Paraverbal therapists help the children in and out of school hours. There are also staff psychologists and psychiatrists. The policy is to admit only children who have a potential of ultimately functioning within the community. Children requiring commitment are not admitted. Children are selected for Paraverbal Communication after a conference with professional members of the staff of the school. The children are then placed in groups of three children, an optimal group consisting of two withdrawn children and one restless child.

The children meet with the Paraverbal therapist for ½ hour, twice a week, for the entire school year. Immediately after the sessions, a record is made of the children's responses and behavior during the session. How the children relate to peers and the therapist and the responses elicited by the structured and unstructured Paraverbal maneuvers and materials are noted. Progress and recommendations are discussed at staff meetings, so that all of the professionals working with the children can coordinate their efforts and work toward common goals.

With retarded children, Paraverbal Communication is used as a therapeutic agent as well as a learning technique. For example, a child can ventilate his anger using a drum and feel less angry and anxious after doing so. With this same drum, he can tap loud, then soft, tap two times, then four times, tap the syllables of his name, and many other words, thereby learning.

Because of the flexibility of techniques available in Paraverbal Communication, it is an excellent and effective approach for working therapeutically in both structured and unstructured situations. For example, it is common for children to change the lyrics of songs metaphorically in accordance with their needs and wishes. They may thus express previously forbidden thoughts and impulses. Thus in "Little David Play on Your Harp," the words, "he killed Goliath and shouted with joy," were changed by one 9-year-old child to,

"I killed Mr. Z and shouted with joy," an expression felt but not previously expressed.

Another latency-age child made use of the folk song, "Nobody Knows the Trouble I've Seen," sung with intense fervor. He recognized through use of the song's words and music his own troubled self and was stimulated to talk about the situation. Often children are too timid, particularly among the retarded, to venture to sing with the therapist. It is for these retarded children especially that percussion instruments are particularly useful, although they are intriguing to all children. Among retarded children, many feel that adults are not to be trusted; that what they, the children say, is often misinterpreted. Rather than dare to put their feelings into words, these children remain silent or become aggressive. With a percussion instrument to communicate their feelings, they feel they are on safe ground. It is the symbolic instruments that talk, rather than themselves.

Then, too, through the use of percussion instruments, the timid retarded child need not even take the responsibility for initiating participation. The inherent quality of an insistent beat produced by the Paraverbal therapist scoops the child into participating. Sometimes the children spontaneously tap a foot or a finger. It can take patient waiting before some retarded children have courage to pick up and use an instrument. However, once they do, they again have the experience of being on safe ground. That is, percussion instruments have no pitch, and so it is impossible for a child to make a mistake when using them.

Together the Paraverbal therapist and the group produce the surge of the beat and the hesitant retarded child is catapulted into participation. The child thus has the immediate satisfaction of having achieved appropriate activity, which is unconsciously reaffirmed by the endlessly repeated beat of the sound maneuvers.

One of the most structured situations develops out of an extremely unstructured use of the drum. Some children, particularly among the retarded, choose just to bang on the drums. By carefully listening, the Paraverbal therapist can catch a pattern in what seem to be random beats. This pattern is then picked up and played by the therapist on her percussion instrument. Sometimes the child recognizes that the therapist is echoing his drum pattern. Sometimes the therapist needs to call it to the child's attention. In either case, great satisfaction is obtained by the retarded child who is accustomed to failure and disapproval. The recognition of his drum pattern creation gives a feeling of mastery, identity, validation, and consequent pleasure. After many such experiences, these timid children begin to create more and more complicated drum beats, which are admired, listened for, played, and experienced, not only by the Paraverbal therapist, but by the group.

The use of dynamics and variations in the playing of the children's drum patterns develop group feelings and control. The children listen to how loud or how soft, how fast, or how slow the creator of a rhythm plays, and thus they are able to play with him. It is equally important that he too, in turn, respects and plays the other children's patterns after they create them. The children learn to discriminate through timbres of the various instruments. Other kinds of learning take place as well. For example, some children have a problem sharing the instruments. Other children need to learn to hold and protect their instruments. Through the structure of the Paraverbal maneuvers and their inherent pleasure, children learn to choose and share.

The percussion instruments have still other functions. Sometimes there is a wide communicative value to their accompaniment to songs. For example, structure develops as one child takes the strong beat while another taps out the melody. Then there is the child who merely uses the percussion instrument to communicate what he feels. All of this, of course, is usually an outgrowth of much earlier exploration and acceptance of the childen's experimentation by the ther-

apist as the children use the instruments with peers, therapist, or individually.

Still another facet of Paraverbal Communication is painting or chalking to symphonic recorded music. The therapist
lays out paper and chalk or finger paints on a table around
which are three chairs. She tells the children that she will
play a record. A colorful rhythmic piece like "March Militaire" is chosen and played. As the rhythmic music begins,
the children are told to close their eyes and move their hands
in the air while keeping the rhythmic pattern. After they
have listened for about a minute, they are told to open their
eyes, take some chalk, and chalk on the paper in a pattern
that comes from chalking in time to the music. They often
need to have a music pattern tapped out or demonstrated to
them before they can begin to chalk to the music. Many
problems, both in expression and in control, come to light
out of this experience. Some children have trouble letting
the sound and rhythm guide the pattern of the chalk. They
also must learn to share colors. Once the children understand what is to take place, the music–painting and –chalking
experiences provide them with great satisfaction. For some,
there is keen sensuous pleasure from the combination of
using color and moving to the rhythmic music. There is satisfaction too in the sight of the unexpected design evoked by
the music. The originality of their creations is of great value
to children who may have heretofore felt that they could not
create anything of value. The fact that there is not an especially "correct" way to chalk, only whatever way the child
himself chalks, is a great comfort to many retarded children. Many children fantasize aloud during or after working
with paint and music. There is often much spontaneous
talk. There are also a few children who at first cannot use
this medium at all. They either won't soil their hands with
colors or find frightening the very freedom this medium of
expression permits. Some of these children take pleasure in
watching others. Then, as they recognize the nonthreaten-

ing and pleasurable situation, they too, participate. Some children simply like to lightly tap an instrument in time with the recording.

Adolescence

The following case histories demonstrate the therapeutic communicative results with three retarded adolescent children. Each child described was part of a Paraverbal group of three children.

G was 15 years old when she first came into Paraverbal Communication. Her mother had been in a mental institution for 2 years prior to G's placement. Her father was an elderly man whose income came from Social Security. One married sister displayed no interest in either G or her younger sister. Another older sister was in a mental institution.

At the early Paraverbal Communication sessions, G revealed herself as an unusually deprived child, timid, repressed, and overeager to comply. In the generally unstructured pleasurable atmosphere, she gradually relaxed. Her voice grew clear and strong. Her mouth relaxed and her eyes would sometimes reflect genuine feeling. Support and stimulation came not only from the therapist, but was also generated by the showing and exchanging of feelings with the group. At first when creative percussion patterns were requested, G feebly clapped together two tiny cymbals or tentatively shook the maracas to the rhythmic response of the group and therapist. Her participation in singing was the same. Her voice was weak, often inaudible. Her facial expression was one of bewilderment or of an eternal tense smiling at the lips, with eyes blank. G hitched onto the words of the folk songs as the simple evocative phrases were contextually repeated in each song that the group sang. At first there were no verbal associations, but later on, dramatic and significant feelings poured forth.

In contrast to her previously timid silence was her poetic and intuitive expression of her own as well as the group's feeling when singing the song "Sometimes I Feel Like a Motherless Child." The therapist had structured this song particularly with G in mind. The song is rhythmic, with repeated phrases and a mournful, yearning tune; the lyrics are, "Sometimes I feel like a motherless child, sometimes I feel like a motherless child, a long ways from home, a long ways from home." When they finished singing, the therapist asked the group, "Who knows what the song means?" G, who would never verbally discuss how she felt, swiftly responded to the question. She said with profound emotion, "Well, it's like when I ride along in the subway and I can't read the signs in the station fast enough and I get scared and I'm afraid I'm lost and I say to myself, 'Momma, Momma, help me.'" She looked at the therapist long, and the others silently nodded, avowing their oneness with her cry.

In the percussion area, where G had participated with the group in a reflex manner with no creativity or abandon at all, she gradually began to experiment while accompanying her favorite songs. She dramatically underscored their meaning with a wide flourish of the maracas or a clash of the tiny cymbals. She began to use her body. Motor skills became freer. The cymbals were raised and clapped over her head, her shoulders moved and swayed rhythmically as the maracas wove their soft rhythm around the songs.

The other two children and the therapist shared astonished and pleased surprise at G's offerings. The more pleased and sharing they all were, the more intricate and creative her expression became. Soon she essayed a new instrument, the castinets—still a small instrument, in keeping with her gentle personality, yet a new means for communication. Now G was really reaching out. She learned to manipulate these clacking instruments with fiery facility. The children began to call them "G's instruments," and, when it was her turn to give an original rhythmic pattern, the children leaned toward her with eager anticipation. The more they admired, the more creative and radiant she became.

One of the social workers came into the room as G happened to be creating a solo castinet pattern. She said to the therapist later, "You know when G was working with those castinets, she looked beautiful." And she did. Her face flushed, her eyes shone. Her head was thrown back like a Spanish dancer. The right hand was held high, the left, low. She was at home and free in a world of sound and movement that she herself was making.

G's growth was even more graphically illustrated in her use of the chalking to rhythmic, symphonic music. When she first started, her deprivation and timidity were all too woefully expressed by meager, dull productions. Her chalk patterns in response to the rhythmic sounds were thin, monotonous, and of one dull tan color. She herself was tense and she constantly looked up from the paper for the therapist's approval. As she learned that all the therapist wanted was for G to chalk onto the drawing paper whatever color or design the music made her feel, she began to get joy from the opportunity presented. Each session her movements became freer. Strokes became bolder and more fanciful. The music charged through her. Eventually her productions became an esthetic delight to behold. Colors were bold or exquisitely delicate as the music suggested. Patterns were balanced, yet free. Often as she worked at her easel, her movements were so free they were like a dance before an altar.

Movement was an effective communication vehicle for her, and it was employed using many other materials and maneuvers. G delighted in dramatizing affect sounds on various instruments and having the other children guess what she was dramatizing. She also enjoyed guessing what other children meant by their movements. She enjoyed rhythmic ball bouncing with the other children and rhythmic pounding of clay. All of these interactive movement maneuvers gave her opportunities to communicate feelings and extend her horizons through Paraverbal Communication. She gained the ability to display a good capacity for friendship and, within her limits, excellent work performance. The next step was providing G with an opportunity to have guidance in job seeking in the community.

W was another retarded adolescent seen in a group situation. When W entered Paraverbal Communication, he was a 13-year-old boy with an I.Q. of 68. The psychologist indicated that this score was probably below his maximum potential. He was passive and withdrew to avoid feelings of inadequacy. He was inhibited, incapable of expressing hostility, and incapable of relating to people. In his social adjustment, he was anxious, dependent, immature, and restless. He made sporadic efforts to behave the way, in his poor judgment, he thought the staff wanted him to behave. He neither knew what he really wanted to do, nor was he able to judge what others really wanted of him. He had difficulty learning anything in school.

Before he came to this facility for retarded youth, he lived with his parents and his two sisters, aged 2 and 3. His mother was compulsive, anxious, and protective. His father was a rigid man who worked as a foreman in the post office. Both parents were disappointed in W and had difficulty accepting his limitations. At first, help was sought at a child guidance clinic. He was diagnosed as schizophrenic and treated for 2 years with no improvement. Help from the guidance center did not produce sufficient improvement for W to remain at home, so the center suggested this placement to be most appropriate.

At W's first Paraverbal Communication session, he was friendly and eager to please. Soon the nonstructured and accepting atmosphere, the singing of lively rhythmic songs, and the insistent rhythmic accompaniment on all drums released him and allowed him to reveal his anxious, chaotic condition. He began to reveal his hostility and restlessness.

At first, he hit and cursed the other children, snarled at the therapist, used obscene language, and beat the drums exuberantly, but often at random. After several months of both sound and movement maneuvers, he found genuine pleasure in the sound of his own voice. He liked to sing alone and shortly, for the first time, communicated the fact that he had feelings similar to those in the song he was unconsciously using metaphorically. W began to get comfort from listening to and singing pertinent lyrics. Songs that were sad songs he called "his" songs. Also, from random pounding, he moved on to real creativity on the drums. At first he would beat out his rage, but gradually he became eager to have the satisfaction that came from the self-created regular rhythms. He translated some of his excitement into movement and the constructive channels of sound dynamics. Spontaneous talk then developed. The opportunity to sing, play, and dramatize his feelings, and to have these feelings understood and accepted by his peers and the therapist gave him new self-respect. He became less anxious, fawning, dependent, restless, and belligerent. He slowly matured. At first he was constantly tardy and made excuses, but later he became prompt and reliable. He openly expressed the wish to be the therapist's son. He now related better to his peers and offered to share instruments with them. The only maneuver to which he did not respond with pleasure was painting and chalking to music. He could not bear to soil his hands with the paint and chalk. During these periods while the other children were painting, he would often softly tap the drum in rhythmic accompaniment to the recording.

At other times, he would get up, seize a piece of clay, and start pounding. As he did so, the therapist would introduce a rhythmic accompaniment on a drum or tambourine to structure his activity. This accompaniment also gave him the feeling that the therapist was interacting with him and understanding what he was doing. At one point, he stopped banging on the clay and started to softly roll it back and forth. He started murmuring. Finally, the therapist was able to catch a few of his words. He said softly, "It's too sad, it's too sad." The therapist did not comment but continued to tap gently with him. After a few minutes, he picked up a puppet that was nearby and started to manipulate it slowly. Then he turned to the therapist and said, "He's sad because he has no one to talk to at home, but here I have you. I can show how I feel." At this point, the therapist said, "What else would you like to use?" He picked up the soap bubbles and handed the bottle to the therapist. "Blow," he said. With this, the therapist blew some bubbles. Then to help channel his feelings, she said to him, "Crack them if you can catch them." He did so and as he clapped and broke each bubble, he looked triumphant. Then the therapist blew some bubbles toward the floor and said, "Maybe you would like to stamp them out." He did so with great glee and a look of mastery could be seen on his face and in his motions. The other children joined him, and they too, had a look of satisfaction and achievement. Then he turned to the therapist and said, "Someday I'd like to go to a music school." The two other children looked surprised. One boy in the group said, "No schools for me." Of course, going to a formal music school was not the Paraverbal goal for W. It was, however, a sign of his wish to be a part of the real outside world where performance and not just verbalization was expected of him. As he continued on in the Paraverbal Communication sessions, he not only used a greater variety of materials, but also through the materials, dramatized and communicated his feelings. He also dramatized the lyrics of some of the songs the therapist had introduced. All three of the boys were intrigued by each others' use of the materials and lyrics. They all achieved improvement in school and in social situations.

A was part of a group of three adolescent boys at the same facility for retarded youth. When A came for Paraverbal Communication, he was 13 years old. His I.Q. was relatively high for a retarded child. He was hyperactive, had a fear of the dark, had nightmares, and had failed at school. He preferred to play with younger children. A had two siblings, a 16-year-old brother and a 2-year-old sister. The brother at one time needed psychiatric help, received it, and made a satisfactory adjustment. His young sister was an anxious child. A's father was tubercular and away from home during A's early childhood. When he returned, the parents quarrelled a good deal. His mother claimed she was the cause of A's difficulties—she gave all her love to other people's children while teaching school because she had had a miscarriage and longed for a baby. She felt A was deprived of her love as well as bewildered by his parents' quarrelling. He was evaluated at a testing center and recommended for psychiatric treatment at the same facility for retarded youth, but he would not cooperate. The psychiatrist then suggested that he come to Paraverbal Communication sessions to see if he could begin to relate to his peers and to determine whether he could learn despite his severe anxiety.

When he first joined the existing group of two boys in the Paraverbal Communication session, he was anxious. A refused to become involved with the materials of the sound and movement maneuvers with the exception of those connected with familiar songs. He responded to the stimulus of the songs' rhythm first. He would move his body, tapping his hands or feet spontaneously in synchrony with the therapist. Eventually, he learned to use these same songs metaphorically to communicate his feelings. At first, his facial expression would merely reflect that of the therapist, then he gradually started responding metaphorically to the content of the song lyrics. He began to communicate by continuously questioning the content of the song lyrics. After this, he began to communicate verbally about the lyrics, which were carefully chosen with his personal interests and needs in mind. He was particularly interested in trains. Meanings of words as well as the stories of the ballads themselves also stimulated him to comment. The free, unstructured, accepting Paraverbal atmosphere where he could wander and/or participate at will seemed to give him the needed feeling of safety and freedom. In contrast to most children, he moved from song lyrics to tentative drumming. However, the steady rhythm of both his peers and the therapist automatically brought him into group participation. He displayed overt physical pleasure when participating in rhythmic body movement. His fear seemed to evaporate. With this security and trust, A was able to make his first request for help—in reading, because of his wish to read the lyrics of the songs that attracted him. Then after a brief period of watching his peers paint to symphonic rhythmic music, he asked for paint and paper. This happened on a day when the recording was very colorful and rhythmic. This maneuver became one of his favorites. The combined sensuality of finger paints and the rhythmic beat of colorful music released his fantasies, which he enjoyed dramatizing. A experienced needed motor release with the painting and concomitantly began to speak freely. There were spontaneous discussions of fantasies, his homelife, and early childhood experiences.

A′s involvement with Paraverbal Communication proved valuable. He learned to relate well to his peers and to the therapist and never had a tantrum during any of the Paraverbal Communication sessions. A made a real effort to behave appropriately like the other boys in the group and expressed a wish to learn and to grow up. He could now benefit from psychiatric treatment.

Summary

In working with retarded children, enabling them to communicate is especially challenging for the therapist. The pleasurable atmosphere and the opportunities to learn by experience through the sensorimotor strategies or maneuvers provide these children with a needed bridge to communication. This then leads to cognitive and behavioral development. The trust these children thus gain with the therapist who permits them choices and accepts all levels of participation, contributes to an amelioration of their cognitive and social problems. The flexibility and wide variety of the Paraverbal maneuvers used to engage children varying in age from 3 years through adolescence stimulate and encourage this growth.

Cooperation on the part of the business and professional world in providing training and jobs for retarded individuals has given encouragement to retarded children, their parents, and the professionals who work with them to develop their optimal potentials.

8

The Autistic Child

Autism is a baffling syndrome that has been studied by many distinguished researchers, including Kanner and Eisenberg, who described it as early as 1943. Currently, the diagnosis of autism as listed in the *Diagnostic and Statistical Manual of Mental Disorders,* Third Edition (1980) is accepted by most professionals. The essential features of children afflicted with this behavioral syndrome are a lack of responsiveness to other human beings, gross impairment in communicative skills, and bizarre responses to various aspects of the environment, all developing within the first 30 months of age. Various combinations of causality fall along a continuum, with largely environmental factors at one end, and inherent or congenitally based vulnerability at the other.

143

This chapter addresses itself particularly to the environmental factors that contribute to autistic behavior.

A major problem that these children have is that they do not communicate, due partly to environmental causes. By providing them with an environment that functions as a bridge to communication, their problem often can be ameliorated. The basic rationale of Paraverbal Communication, acceptance and ongoing pleasure in the therapeutic environment, addresses the essential problems of autism. The mostly sensorimotor approach used in the Paraverbal Communication maneuvers permits the construction of the needed bridge to communication for the autistic child. The use of sound other than verbal is of special value with these children, who characteristically do not respond to speech. What they do respond to at first in the Paraverbal maneuvers are nonverbal vocalizations and statements in the form of rhymes and speech cadences, whether in chanting, in singing, or on instruments that often accompany the vocalizations. Paraverbal Communication begins by attempting to involve the autistic child through familiar song melodies, miming motor activity, tones of percussion and stringed instruments, painting and chalking to music, and other media in a nonverbal dialogue with the therapist and, when feasible, with the mother. As the child develops, verbal communication is introduced and increased. The work is based on the dynamic consideration that the autistic child is overwhelmed by painful affect, which causes him to withdraw. The crippling effect of the painful anxiety is reduced by the introduction and substitution of the pleasurable affect. This is formed largely for the autistic child through familiar repeated percussive sounds and pleasurable rhythmic chanting accompanied by simple movements. The pleasurable sound and movement interactions command his attention. With his attention captured, the child can more easily relate and be part of the real world.

The basis of some of the Paraverbal techniques used in

working with the autistic child are extrapolated from Anna Freud's ideas for preanalytic treatment of children (1946). She stresses two basic points: first the child requires his own childish peculiarities to be appropriately matched; second one must always establish a very definite emotional relationship with the child. Both of these significant ideas are readily implemented through the flexible, pleasurable use of the maneuvers. Regarding the first point, the wide variety of novel sensorimotor choices provides such matching possibilities using careful consideration of the child's own unique behavior. In the course of using the sound maneuvers, touch, hand gestures, facial expression, marked tonal changes in voice, and the various sounds issuing from the instruments are all used to engage and involve the autistic child. In the traditional therapeutic setting, the autistic child falls apart and excludes speech addressed to him. However, when packaged in the various sound and movement maneuvers that function as a substitute for ordinary speech, the autistic child is more able to communicate. To maintain the requisite pleasurable atmosphere, the therapist needs to carefully observe and judge the reactions and responses of the autistic child to the sensorimotor approach, both sound and movement. Does the child smile or perhaps laugh? If so, the maneuver is continued. Does he even for a moment show fleeting signs of falling apart? Then the therapist promptly substitutes a new maneuver or returns to one that gave pleasure earlier. In this regard, it is important for the therapist to be aware that sometimes as many as 15 alternate maneuver changes need to be made in a ½-hour session to insure that consistent pleasure prevails and that contact is maintained.

As the child interacts with the therapist and/or his mother using the pleasurable movement maneuvers, he becomes desensitized to speech, and is less anxious. In later sessions as the therapy proceeds, there is an occasional maneuver that the child enjoys for as long as 5 or even 10 minutes. This is all valuable provided the child does not prolong and intensify that particular involvement to the point that he himself becomes exclusively involved with the sensorimotor medium to the exclusion of the therapist and/or his mother. If this inappropriate but characteristic situation is allowed, the basic concept of reciprocal pleasurable communication is destroyed. It is therefore the therapist's responsibility to forestall this possible withdrawal by introducing other therapeutic interventions. These can involve change of tempo, pitch, or accent, in order to refocus and maintain the child's attention and thereby continue the interactive aspect of the therapy, which leads to the desired communication.

Should the introduction of these stimuli not achieve the attention and reciprocity basic to the method, the therapist introduces an alternate, sharply contrasting maneuver as described in the case study on page 147.

In using the sound and movement maneuvers to achieve communication, touch plays a major role in the strategic use of the different sensorimotor tools that are employed. Many of its functions are similar to those described by Frank (1957) in his article on tactile experience. He discussed the confidence and gratification the infant obtains from frequent parental touching and the fact that the tactile experience is reciprocal (what a person touches also touches him). Frank further explained that touch is a route to establishing intimacy and the arousal of feelings, both of which are needed in reaching the autistic child. With this in mind, throughout all maneuvers, occasion should be found to appropriately touch the child and thus reassure him and tangibly communicate meaning and feelings. At times, the child spontaneously touches the therapist. As the child progresses, he needs less of the sensorimotor stimuli used in the maneuvers (Heimlich 1972), stimuli that have been used to help desensitize him in his acute anxiety. The tactile experience so inherent in Paraverbal Communication serves as a pleasurable bridge to the treatment goals for the autistic child, which are improved responsiveness to other human beings and better communicative skills (social and cognitive) (Simon 1988). Examples of the use of these techniques are presented in the following case study.

Case Study

History

B is a handsome little boy, 3 years, 4 months old. His parents first became concerned about his deviant behavior when he was 2 years old. Among other atypical behavior, he was excessively anxious. Even though he clung to his mother, he did not respond when she spoke to him or when she tried to play with him. He was equally indifferent to all other people, including his father, his 6-year-old sister, and his two teenage stepbrothers. Additionally, his inability to communicate was apparent both in his stereotypical gestures and meaningless use of words. For example, he would stand still, then flap his hands and gaze at them. Sometimes he would repeatedly murmur the phrase "13 arches" without any specific reference to its meaning. His behavior with regard to the physical environment was equally strange. On entering an apartment house, he would insist on numbering every single door he passed. In his own house he demanded that the furniture, decorations, and appliances be always in exactly the same place.

B had received extensive diagnostic examinations by several doctors. Neurological examination had revealed central nervous system dysfunction, contributing to his poor response to auditory and visual stimulation, poor articulation, and developmental difficulties of motor coordination. The results of intellectual testing were uncertain, partially due to B's lack of cooperation. The examiner suggested a diagnosis of possible functional retardation. The psychiatrist to whom B was referred felt he would best respond to Paraverbal Communication because of the variety of novel and flexibly utilized sensorimotor approaches. B's anomalies were characteristic of autism. As defined by Howlin and Rutter (1987) the essential characteristics of autism are: (1) impairment in human relatedness; (2) impairment in language, ranging from absence of speech to bizarre and deviant language patterns; (3) peculiar motor behavior, ranging from stereotypes to more complex behavioral repetition; and (4) early onset, before 30 months of age. In addition, B exhibited the specific characteristics of autism described by Kanner (1958), Kanner and Eisenberg (1955), and Creak (1963), that is, gaze avoidance, an unusual sensitivity to loud sounds, pronoun reversal, and acute, excessive, and seemingly illogical anxiety.

Paraverbal Communication with B

He entered the therapy room clinging to his mother, his eyes downcast. Two chairs, a large floor drum, and an autoharp were placed in the room. In addition, several percussion and string instruments lay under a cloth on a table close by for possible later use. A chair for the ..other was placed in a far corner near the door so she could leave the session when B was sufficiently involved with his newfound pleasures. This was to facilitate separation with a minimum of anxiety. The therapist greeted them both and tapped the drum while B's mother removed his jacket. B looked up briefly. The therapist smiled, then went over and took B's hand, seated him opposite her, knee to knee and tapped the drum that was close by. The therapist tapped the drum again, and this time, of his own accord, he promptly struck it also. This was the first step toward nonverbal, pleasurable communication and relationship. The therapist immediately tapped the drum again, this time in imitation of B's tap to validate his rhythmic offering. Her immediate response also sustained his attention. For variety and stimulation, she tapped a little louder than he. His response was to make whimpering sounds and try to slide off the chair.

The therapist then attempted to re-engage B by substituting a different instrument—an autoharp. Both its sound and its shape were in sharp contrast to the drum. She placed the autoharp partly on his knees and partly on hers, so that he could share the vibrations as she rhythmically strummed the instrument. The propinquity also permitted her to control his movements so the session would not be interrupted by his restlessness. First, with one of her fingers she plucked the strings to engage his attention and at the same time give him the pleasure of the new sound. He promptly imitated her. She smiled and said, "Oh, B, what a lovely sound you made!" He seemed pleased at this approval. He touched the strings again. Then, as B continued to imitate her for a very brief period, they alternately plucked the strings.

Thus their relationship was developed a little further through reciprocity and pleasure in a nonverbal dialogue conducted through alternating sounds. It was both a beginning in the direction of extending his attention span and another small step toward communication. The therapist then began to continuously chant B's name while they took turns plucking the autoharp. The chant, to the tune "Frère Jacques," went as follows: "I like B, I like B, he is good, he is nice," and so on. This technique was used as still another stepping stone in the building of their relationship as well as for language development. Not until the therapist chanted "B" for the tenth time did he acknowledge his pleasure in the personal, verbal focus of their reciprocal involvement. He looked directly into the therapist's eyes, smiled, and spontaneously chanted "B." However, this verbal step forward was ended almost as quickly as it had begun. The therapist had to substitute a new pleasure immediately to maintain his attention and involvement.

No sooner had he said his name than he quickly slid to the floor. Observing this regressed position, the therapist introduced a new strategy with the emphasis on pleasure through touch, body movement, and concrete, descriptive chants (Stern 1985). (Stern [1985] stresses the importance and value of the intimacy that develops through touch and close physical contact of mother and child. Stern refers to Freud's comments on tactile sensation associated with pleasure.) What she did was to grab both his legs and begin rhythmically moving them so that his knees bent upward toward his abdomen; then she straightened them out. She alternated this movement with rhythmically stretching his legs out to form a V, and moving them together again. Simultaneously, she improvised a melody with lyrics that described what they were doing. The lyrics were "pushing, pushing, back and forth, pushing, pushing, in and out." This was a slightly more complex and sophisticated means of communicating with him than the means she had used before. The new strategy not only involved touch, rhythmic body movement, and repeated use of his name, but in addition used repeated, chanted words describing directional movement. He showed his pleasure by the increasingly responsive ease in his body movement and by his continued smiling. His attention span this time was slightly longer than in the previous interchanges. However, after 3 minutes he pulled his feet away from the therapist's hands, got up, and went to look for his mother, who had left the room.

When they returned together, the therapist included her in the session. Inclusion of the mother is desirable, but not a necessary part of the therapy. The session continued with B facing the therapist while sitting in his mother's lap. In this new situation the therapist introduced a variation of the first simple procedure (alternate rhythmic tapping). This time she used a small, brightly colored metal xylophone on which a mallet was used in turn by B, his mother, and the therapist to produce sound. The purpose of arousing and engaging him by means of the sight and sound of a new percussive instrument was not only to help extend his attention span and continue his pleasure, but also to help him with his problem of auditory and visual avoidance.

With B's involvement in this maneuver, the first session ended. Both mother and child were pleased and smiling. What is significant about this session is that communication (a prime factor in behavioral change) was initiated. It could be observed by the following behavior on B's part:

1. B responded to the therapist—a beginning toward responsiveness to another human being
2. B participated in the maneuvers with the therapist—a step toward improvement in communication skills
3. B imitated the therapist—a movement toward appropriate response to another human being and to the environment
4. B spoke his name—a step toward communication
5. B used material appropriately—a bridge to appropriate response to the environment
6. B smiled—another sign of the beginning of a relationship with the therapist and her pleasureful and accepting approach

Communication was able to occur because of the following:

1. The therapist was alert to changes in the child's attention or reaction and immediately substituted an alternate, pleasurable procedure
2. The therapist used a variety of channels for communication to fit the child's response
3. The therapist and B interacted as a unit
4. The therapist did not tell the child to do anything
5. The therapist did not ask the child anything

The sessions that followed concentrated on continuing the patient's pleasure in the paraverbal maneuvers and were held twice a week. Each session produced some slight progress in B's ability and willingness to communicate. At first this progress was mostly on the nonverbal level. It could be observed in the aggressive way he began to strike the percussion instruments. Sometimes he would glance over at the therapist as he struck them. Progress was also noted in B's behavior and the use of his body; for instance, instead of limp, random motions, he now responded with more purposeful body movement. The structure of the rhythms encouraged this. The purposefulness of his movements now helped him indicate what he wanted or how he felt. In the course of this development, he himself began to recognize what he was capable of doing and how he was able to communicate both with his body and with the materials he used. His attention span began to show signs of expanding. In addition, he showed somewhat increased spontaneity, curiosity, and more intense, appropriate exploration of the materials and environment around him. His development was indicative of a personal observation made by Bender (1952) regarding the close relationship found between motility, the emotional state, and the ideation of the child and the need for a conscious effort at integrating these components. In addition to B's increased nonverbal facility, the therapist could also observe some progress in his ability to imitate changed descriptive words.

From simple verbal imitation he progressed to imitating phrases and sentences. For example, the therapist would chant and dramatize the following hide-and-seek lyrics: "Where, oh where is mommy?" B soon learned to imitate the words and then to spontaneously point and answer, "There she is!" This event was followed by much role changing and new words to fit new situations; for example, "Where, oh where is B?" Many similar strategies were used over and over again. Besides language development, the therapist now could observe improved behavior in two other areas. One was B's decreased anxiety in connection with loud sounds (Escalona and Bergman 1949). The other was his decreased anxiety in separating from his mother (Mahler 1975). Many similar hide-and-seek strategies and other pleasurable sensorimotor experiences described later were specifically introduced to help him with his inadequate development in the separation–individuation process. With this significant development he was on his way to what Mahler (1975) terms "object constancy." The mother was now free to leave the room whenever the therapist did not need her as part of the therapeutic work. (Incidentally, the mother was able to report decreased separation anxiety both at home and at school.) By the fourteenth session, B was able to verbalize spontaneously in a three-word phrase what he wanted. He said, "Want this now," and reached for the autoharp. Up to this point, it had always been the therapist who introduced the various tools for communication, although she always gave B the pleasure of using tools any way he chose. For example, he could use them loud or soft, fast or slow, and for as long or short a time as he wished. This technique helped him in the following ways: (1) using the tools as he chose gave him a sense of power and identity; (2) a feeling of acceptance promoted his relationship with the therapist; and (3) a sense of independence was developed which helped him communicate better, both nonverbally and, eventually, verbally.

At this point, the therapist noticed a marked increase in assertive and aggressive behavior. Once, for example, when the therapist tried to substitute a new maneuver and new material to head off his burgeoning repetitiveness, she deliberately hid what he was using. He got up, grabbed the instrument and sat on it, and defiantly refused to give it up. It was at this point that B took a major therapeutic step forward by verbally communicating his anger at the therapist's interference. He stamped his foot and yelled, "Quiet!" The therapist encouraged this newfound style of behavior and said, "Okay, B, maybe later on you'll want to use different things."

At the next session, she concealed all the instruments to obviate any chance of his resuming his repetitive, solitary tapping behavior of the previous session. When he came in she took his hand, pointed to the brilliant finger paints displayed near the easel, and chanted challengingly and with a smile on her face, "Look what I can do, you can do it too!" She then threw several blobs of finger paint on the paper clipped to the easel and gayly smeared one of the blobs over the paper. She chanted, "Catch the paint, B, catch it before it falls on the floor!" This strategy was aimed at substituting a constructive pleasure for his destructive, isolating, repetitive behavior of the previous session. B grabbed the finger paint and smeared it on the paper for a brief period and responded rhythmically and pleasurably to the therapist's interactive chanting of "Round and round, and up and down on the paper we go." Then after a few minutes of intense absorption and delight in what he was doing, he suddenly stopped. He turned to his mommy who was nearby watching, and said, "Wash hands, wash hands, wash hands!" The therapist took the cue and immediately changed her tack. Taking his hand, she promptly took him to the basin.

In doing this, she had two purposes in mind: (1) to gratify B's immediate needs and (2) to take this opportunity for them to develop water as a substitute therapeutic medium of pleasure and growth. At the basin after washing his hands, they engaged in lots of rollicking, splashing, and floating of soap. The taps were turned on and off slow and fast, and at B's request the basin was emptied and filled over and over again. The therapist accompanied these activities with rhythmic, chanted descriptions of what they were doing. The pleasurable aftermath and excitement of the waterplay seemed to counteract B's sudden distaste for fingerpaint on his hands. It now became an endless source of pleasure and learning for him. He loved the experience of turning the faucets on and off and washing the paint off his hands. In later sessions, water was the prime medium of pleasure and learning. After entering the room for his session, B said what he continued to say for many sessions following: "Fun with finger paint!" or "Want finger paint!" He then proceeded to squeeze, rub, and mix the finger paint. All this was done to the organizing stimulus of the theapist's rhythmically chanted descriptions of what they were doing. Whenever the therapist thought that B seemed about to lose interest in the finger painting, she would suggest they go to the basin; once there, water became a substitute medium for his pleasure and development, although the finger painting retained its appeal. Taking turns and sometimes together, they would just pour water into the basin or later on would float various objects in it. In this way, new feelings about what they were doing were communicated, and new words were used as B became increasingly involved in the many ways he could use the water. Then, once again, aggression would come to the fore.

It could be first observed in the aggressive manner with which he used the water medium. He would deliberately turn the faucet on much too powerfully or would vigorously splash the water so that some would spill on the floor. When this happened, the therapist would continue chanting a description of what he was doing. On one such occasion, he laughed aloud and looked at her defiantly, saying in a clear, whole sentence, "Look, look, it's on the floor!" The therapist smiled and pretended to look shocked. Then with good humour but firmly involving him in reality she said, "Come on, B, you help me mop it up." They mopped up the floor together until it was dry. After this comment and shared clean-up meant to involve B in responsive behavior, the therapist felt it was necessary to quickly provide B with a new pleasurable but more structured interaction lest he become too anxious.

The therapist asked B's mother to join them in a circle. She put the drum in the center of the floor, grasped B with one hand and had his mother take the other. Following this, she took the mother's free hand so that the three of them formed a circle around the drum. Then she slowly repeated a descriptive chant, "B goes round the drum, Mommy goes round the drum, we go round the drum, boom!" This was immediately followed by all three dropping to the floor at the accented word "boom." There was laughter from everyone after the sudden explosive sound of "boom" and the quick, regressive change in body position to the floor. B loved it and requested that it be done over and over again.

Altogether B attended 74 sessions. Each lasted from 30 to 45 minutes; they were held twice a week. B's autistic problems were dealt with through a series of Paraverbal maneuvers. Treatment was based on the dynamic consideration that the autistic child is overwhelmed by the painful affect that causes him to withdraw. The substitution of pleasurable affect based on the therapeutic use of rhythmic sound and movement interchanges, and a minimal use of direct speech, reduced the painful affect and made appropriate communication possible.

Both child and therapist (and, when appropriate, the mother) were involved in a variety of these maneuvers. All the maneuvers used had something in common: (1) they were pleasureful; (2) they aroused attention through the properties inherent in the sonorities (vocal or instrumental) that are the integral part of all maneuvers, including rhythmic body movement, painting, and waterplay. They were always used for interactive communication among child, therapist, and mother when she was present at the sessions.

The sensorimotor tools for communication and the pleasurable and accepting way they were used led to increased communication, the lessening of autistic behavior, and eventual moderate improvement.

The techniques that were used with B could be regarded as similar to or like a recapitulation of the mother–infant behavior described by Stern (1974). He suggests that there is a "mutual maintenance of a level of attention and arousal." The Paraverbal therapist and/or mother provide "a continually changing array of sounds, motions, facial expressions, and tactile and kinesthetic events." B's was one of

12 cases of children diagnosed as autistic using the *Diagnostic and Statistical Manual of Mental Disorders* (1980) criteria and treated with Paraverbal Communication therapy. Nine of the children were patients at a psychiatric facility; three were treated privately.

Summary

Paraverbal Communication with its sensorimotor interaction is an alternate approach to the treatment of autistic children. Criteria for autism presented are gauged according to the *Diagnostic and Statistical Manual of Mental Disorders* (1980).

The treatment approach is based on the theory that (1) the autistic child is overwhelmed by painful affect and (2) the introduction and substitution of pleasurable affect, and the avoidance whenever possible of direct speech, can be used to reduce the crippling outcome of painful affect characteristic of autism.

Arousal is the first step toward responsiveness to the therapist and always occurs in the first session. The next step in behavioral progress, imitation of the therapist, has the following therapeutic significances: it is (1) a slightly more complex response; (2) the beginning of more appropriate use of the materials and the environment by the child; (3) a nonverbal way of communicating with the therapist; and also (4) a pleasurable beginning of reciprocal behavior.

9

Metaphoric Lyrics as a Bridge to the Adolescent's World

This chapter discusses the Paraverbal metaphoric use of rock music lyrics to help hard-to-reach adolescents communicate feelings about their roles in society and their own development. The rationale underlying the method is that if the adolescent can feel accepted and be engaged through means that are familiar and pleasurable, he can learn to trust, ventilate feelings, and communicate. Through guided discussion about familiar lyrics and isues they evoke, adolescents begin to offer their opinions, listen to others' ideas, and learn to disagree without being aggressive. They begin to discuss ways to gain control over their lives and learn the advantages of becoming disciplined participants in society. They begin to consider and learn alternatives for coping with their daily pressures, rather than falling victim to a rock idol's solution, which is frequently withdrawal from society or aggression toward it. They begin to communicate.

Working with a group of alienated adolescents is both challenging and instructive. It is challenging because of the nature of the adolescent—his strong idealism on the one hand and on the other his capacity to change his mind and embrace new ideas once convinced of their relevance. It is instructive because professionals working with adolescents can learn from their eagerness to discuss their own developmental and societal issues and then guide them concerning their fit in today's world. Erikson (1963) discusses role confusion and adolescents' need to "keep themselves together by temporarily over-identifying, to the apparent complete loss of identity, with heroes of cliques and crowds." These identity issues, hidden amidst layers of instrumental and vocal sound, are the very ones being voiced in many popular songs today. By enabling the adolescent to refer to messages he considers important, sung by his heroes and about his world, therapists can become meaningfully involved with the adolescent by understanding him at a much deeper level.

Popular lyrics are utilized for two reasons. Adolescents readily accept the messages in the songs and feel comfortable and competent communicating in this familiar medium. High interest in the music is already established and the specific vocabulary and language are thoroughly understood. Song lyrics, although verbal, are not identical with speech. They are a unique, pleasurable medium combining attractive stimuli of the repetition inherent in rhyme, rhythm, and music. Involvement with these rock lyrics helps adolescents to feel in control when the accepting therapist permits them to select the songs that appeal to them. In addition, this medium is predictable to the adolescent. Popular rock songs are in themselves predictable because they are already formulated and heard again and again. Relevant adolescent themes in songs develop into meaningful communication and the issues stated in the lyrics can be identified, challenged or supported, and interpreted. The second advantage of using lyrics with adolescents is that they are able to talk about the experiences in the lyrics, thereby distancing themselves safely from conflicts they may themselves feel but are unprepared to address. Saari (1986), in her discussion of therapeutic communication with adolescents, states, "Developmentally they are, and consider themselves to be, too old for play therapy and yet they are not truly capable of dealing with their problems purely through a direct discussion as is expected of adults." The Paraverbal use of metaphor inherent in the lyrics therefore enables adolescents to discuss relevant issues that might be threatening in many ways if directly confronted.

Rock music reaches 66.5 million people under 19 in the United States. Between 7th and 12th grades, adolescents spend approximately 10,500 hours listening to rock music, only 500 hours less than the total amount spent in class over the 12 school years (Fischer and Herkes 1985). Adolescents have designated as their spokesmen the recording stars who sing and provide information about the world, tell about relationships, instruct, and often promise instant relief from difficult life situations.

Lyrics are more controversial today than in the past 20 years because the recording stars themselves decide on the content of the songs they sing. This was not the case earlier when powerful industry censors and recording companies exerted more control over songs they would promote (Hirsch 1971).

The songs and messages, today as in the past, help solidify adolescents' identities by providing them with instant recognition and a concept of themselves in the future which is very often lacking in troubled young people. Lyrics frequently describe harsh requirements for today's youth. Their resistant behavior appears to be a way of protecting their separateness and independence and their struggle for meeting life's requirements. Frequently, lyrics instruct listeners to adopt violence as the solution to situations that can better be handled in other ways. Because adolescents are so readily influenced by their rock idols' solutions for gaining independence, the need is great to develop adolescents' abilities to question these messages before accepting and following them. When offered opportunities to discuss their independence among peers using their own media with professional steering, adolescents experience the benefits of communication.

Different themes appeal to different adolescents, but the common denominator appears to be the "most popular" songs (Cole 1971). Many of these songs describe a threatening world full of unrealistic and demanding expectations. The manner of coping with this difficult world is often short-sighted—withdrawal or aggression. Alienated adolescents often develop these behavioral extremes after experiencing frequent failure both in school and at home. Gardner (1971) believes that many children who have experienced or observed an excess of traumatic incidents in their first 6 years of life develop a "learned" fear. This learned fear greatly affects one's innate curiosity or learning drive in disastrous ways—evoking helplessness, hopelessness, expectations of failure, and punishment. Therefore, aggression or withdrawal are seen as the only alternatives. Unfortunately, both ways are counterproductive to developing healthy problem-solving skills for successful living.

Realizing then, that the metaphor inherent in popular music was helping adolescents to explain their own situations, wishes, and fears, the therapist applied the Paraverbal metaphoric use of lyrics of popular songs as the vehicle for a group of adolescent boys to begin to communicate. The therapist first recorded current music that was popular among adolescents and transcribed the lyrics. While listening to the music, it is important for each student to have the printed lyrics in front of him. Students are sometimes surprised when confronted by the whole message of a song and often admit to knowing only phrases or certain parts. After a specific song is played, group members are encouraged by the therapist to identify the overall message. It is interesting to hear the variety of ideas offered. A song might have a different meaning for each student, according to his own development, and communication begins when students confront each other about the various ideas. They include feelings regarding pressures, disloyalty of friends, family difficulties, drugs, love, sex, independence, fear (e.g., of violence, nuclear war, AIDS), situations beyond their control, rejection, and not knowing where one belongs. A major theme in today's rock songs consists of the need and ways to escape fears and pressures. Again, this is where therapists can provide guidance that adolescents so badly require at this time. Alternative ways of coping can be considered by drawing the adolescents into the discussion and encouraging them to consider advantages and disadvantages of particular coping mechanisms.

Adolescents are eager to show an understanding of their media and speak up about issues addressed in the songs. The therapist's role is to help expand the adolescent's media to consider solutions after the adolescent has stated the problems. Redl (1966) discusses the ways the adolescent's ego strengthens as he begins to perceive, assess, and predict about social and physical realities. The lyrics create common ground for adolescent and adult and prevent what Redl calls taboos against the out group.

Adolescents want to discuss society and how difficult it is to feel at ease in it. Coles (1986) writes about ways in which children use their nation's traditions and experiences to help construct their own personalities. Many alienated adolescents' experiences include poverty and prejudice; their ideas about their nation and their environment therefore can be nothing more than their own experiences.

Through popular, relevant lyrics, adolescents can first talk about the experience as sung by the performer(s) and

exchange options. An exciting result of this is the adolescents' ability to then talk about their own experiences which
may parallel those of the performers. Adolescents, given the
opportunity to ventilate their feelings, begin to feel less
alienated and more connected to the world around them.
Through the Paraverbal metaphoric use of the lyrics as a
bridge to their own feelings, students were encouraged to
discuss the many anxieties and fears, for example, of nuclear war after listening to and interpreting the lyrics of the
song called "Russians" by Sting.

> In Europe and America, there's a growing feeling of
> hysteria
> Conditioned to respond to all the threats
> And the rhetorical speeches of the Soviets
> Mr. Khruschev said he will bury you; I don't subscribe
> to his point of view
> Such an ignorant thing to do; if the Russians love their
> children too
> How can I save my little boy from Oppenheimer's
> deadly toy
> There isn't a monopoly of common sense on either
> side of the political fence
> We share the same biology, regardless of ideology
> Believe me when I say to you, I hope the Russians love
> their children too
> There is no historical precedent to put words in the
> mouth of the President
> There's no such thing as a winnable way; it's a lie we
> don't believe anymore

As is apparent from the words in the song, many relevant
issues can be discussed and opinions of the adolescents elicited, challenged, supported, but above all, valued. Real
learning takes place when feelings are communicated.

Focusing on feelings is one of many developmental
areas that become structured and manageable through the
metaphoric use of lyrics. The therapist found it important to
ask adolescents to identify and actually label the possible

feelings the singers were communicating through song. Adolescents readily name angry, sad, hurt, restless, nervous, frustrated, weak, sick, sorry, tired, and frightened among others. The therapist can then elicit from the group life situations that bring about similar feelings in themselves. Many adolescents are not in touch with their own feelings and may believe they are losing face when revealing what they feel. Because of the bridging effect of the lyrics, adolescents generally feel free to share their opinions. The metaphor provides "psychic distance from conflicts lest these conflicts become too overwhelming to the sense of the capacity to cope" (Saari 1986).

Another area that is easily developed after listening to specific songs is family relationships. Discussion of the adolescent's position in the family is often significant for him. An oldest child may feel pressure from others' great expectations of him. Having the opportunity for someone else to recognize this pressure and to discuss it often relieves the adolescent. He has the chance to hear other oldest children tell about their situations and how they handle them. The same type of exchange can occur by focusing on pressures of being the youngest or middle child. Pressures to achieve or fulfill expectations are discussed with peers sharing many ideas. As adolescents share common experiences and feelings, they break down the barriers of isolation. A song that is effective in eliciting communication concerning expectations is "Be Good Johnny" by Men at Work.

> Skip, skip, skip, up the road, off to school you go
> Don't be a bad boy, Johnny. Don't you slip up or play
> the fool
> Oh no Ma, oh no Da, I'll be your golden boy
> I will obey every golden rule
> Get taught by the teacher, not to daydream
> And don't mind my brother,
> begoodbegoodbegoodbegood—
> Johnny

A song that directly addresses pressure is entitled "Pressure" by Billy Joel.

> You have to learn to pace yourself—pressure
> You're just like everybody else—pressure
> You've only had to run so far, so good
> But you will come to a place where the only thing
> you'll feel
> Are loaded guns in your face and you'll have to deal
> with—pressure

Questions can be asked about pressure in general. (What do you think pressure means?) Afterward, more direct questioning can begin. (What are some pressures youth your age feel?)

The therapist must be sensitive to the needs of the adolescents and choose songs that address these needs. The adolescents themselves can be the therapist's most valuable resource for specific songs which address relevant issues. Valuable communication is established as the adolescents assist the therapist with songs and, in turn, receive help in having their problems clarified.

Adolescents thoroughly enjoy discussing their own development. Their identities are solidified while brainstorming about the role of an adolescent. What are their roles in life between ages 13 and 19? Life stages and roles can be reviewed beginning with early childhood, elementary school, junior high school, high school, and so on.

A current song called "Growing Up" by Whodini addresses many issues that adolescents enjoy discussing.

> It's all just a part of growing up
> Things are gonna be hard but don't give up
> Oh, growing up is a hell of a job
> The pay is good but the work is hard
> But sometimes you feel like you're gonna quit
> And that's when you remember this
> There ain't nothing new under the sun
> What you're doin now's already been done

> Tug-o-war, blind-man's bluff
> That's just what it's like when you're growing up
> When I was 10, I used to say I was 12
> When I turned 15, I turned bad as Hell
> When I get fed up, all I do is shout
> I may be down but I'm not knocked out

After listening to and offering opinions on the lyrics, adolescents are able to respond to questions such as, What kinds of things are difficult while you are growing up? What does it mean to give up? When are some times when we may give up? Why would a 10-year-old say he was 12? When a person is fed up, what kinds of things can he or she do to get help?

Many songs include lyrics pertaining to childhood and evoke feelings adolescents will address such as "Comfortably Numb" by Pink Floyd.

> I caught a fleeting glimpse out of the corner of my eye
> I turned to look but it was gone
> I cannot put my finger on it now
> The child is grown, the dream is gone, and I have
> become
> Comfortably numb

These lyrics enable the therapist to ask what it is like to have one's feelings numbed and encourage the adolescents to talk about reasons and times one does not want to be in touch with real feelings. This topic is addressed in depth in an article entitled "Adolescents Discuss Themselves and Drugs Through Music" (Mark 1986).

"Another Brick in the Wall," also by Pink Floyd, addresses issues adolescents enjoy discussing such as rejection, loneliness, being misunderstood, wishes for independence, and feelings of alienation.

> Daddy's flown across the ocean, leavin' just a memory
> A snap shot in the family album
> Daddy, what else did you leave for me
> All in all, it was just a brick in the wall

All in all, it was all just bricks in the wall
We don't need no education. We don't need no
thought control
No dark sarcasm in the classroom
Teachers, leave the kids alone
I don't need no arms around me
I don't need no drugs to calm me
I have seen the writing on the wall
Don't think I need anything at all
All in all, you were all just bricks in the wall

Adolescents respond to memories of their childhood and often speak of remorse over lost opportunities and the realities of growing up. Adolescents are eager to have input from those they respect regarding the future and their roles in society. A song that addresses jobs, satisfaction, and survival is "In the 80's" by Crosby, Stills, and Nash

Tired of working, it's going too slow
You just had to be there, but you hated to go
Down to the job where it all feels the same
Thousands of people looking for someone to blame
You and me have got to survive
We'll be lucky if we survive
In the 80's we must come alive
You're part of the country so you put in your claim
They take your identity and they give you a name
They hand you a number and they tell you to wait
They ask you to come inside while they're closing the
gate

Very pertinent to growing up is the issue of independence. The therapist can initiate discussion regarding rights versus privileges of adolescents and rights versus privileges of parents. Guided by a knowledgable therapist, this type of discussion is most productive and enables adolescents to think about their own independence in an objective manner.

After listening to songs about desire for independence, therapists can prepare questions and ask adolescents to write their responses about the rights and privileges in their families. First they make a list of things they think should be a parent's rights in a family. Some typical responses are: "tell you when to come in," "know where kids are going to be at night," "when to go to bed," "not to do drugs," "tell you to do chores," "tell you to go to school," "get respect from your child." Then adolescents can be asked to think about their own rights. Some responses include: "listen to music," "choose your own friends," "privacy," "to dress how you feel," "choose your own profession," and "get respect from your parents." Adolescents can be asked to list some things they consider to be privileges they have or would like to have in their homes. They can be asked about the differences between a right and a privilege.

The therapist can create questions about specific songs or issues, for example, "How we relate to lyrics depends on our personal experiences. Do you agree? Why or why not?" A statement that evokes discussion might be, "The decade of the 90's is filled with many difficult issues. What are some of these issues?" A therapist can provide structure for the adolescents to more affectively respond by empowering them to create their own lyrics, for example, "The song that best describes how I feel is _____. If I were to write a song, the title would be _____ and the first line of the song would be _____." Each popular song is full of adolescent issues and only requires sensitive questioning to encourage these young people to comment on their world, engage in meaningful communication, and consider appropriate alternatives.

Another valuable use of rock lyrics for addressing family matters is to explore music from other decades. It might be relevant to choose the decade in which parents of the adolescents were teenagers. The adolescents can listen to the songs and read the lyrics. The therapist can question the group about issues in the songs. Many adolescents in the group shared definite opinions of the dated music and stated that the issues of the 50's and 60's songs are too sim-

ple and unrealistic. "To the Aisle," a song from this period
of time illustrates the point the adolescents frequently made.

> First a boy and a girl meet each other
> And they sit down and talk for awhile
> In your heart you'll want her for a lover
> While each step draws you closer to the aisle
> Then you put a ring on her finger
> And the tears start flowing a-while
> Then you know she's yours forever
> While each step draws you closer to the aisle

Group members took differing positions on love and
marriage but generally agreed that good relationships didn't
just happen; nor did they usually last forever. Their own
difficult family experiences had taught them the reality of
fleeting relationships and sadness. The lyrics enabled the
adolescents to begin to talk, first about the differences between the lyrics and issues of the two decades and then their
own feelings regarding important relationships.

On the other hand, School Days, by Chuck Berry, shows
today's adolescents that their parents had similar feelings
about school and their own freedom.

> Up in the morning and out to school
> The teacher is teaching the golden rule
> American history and practical math
> You study them hard and hoping to pass
> Working your finger right down to the bone
> The guy behind you won't leave you alone
> As soon as 3 o'clock rolls around
> You finally lay your burden down
> Throw back your books, get out of your seat
> Down the halls and into the street
> Up to the corner and round the bend
> Right to the juke joint, you go in

By using lyrics to educate the adolescents about some of
the issues being sung about during their parents' growing
up years, therapists can encourage a better understanding

of parents' attitudes formed during those years. This experience is often the first time adolescents have considered and begin to understand the society their parents had to face. Adolescents eagerly talk about differences of opinion and behavior between themselves and their parents and appear to gain new insight into their relationships. Coles (1986) explains how some children learn from their fathers' experiences, and why they think and act as they do. This contrasts with many of today's adolescents who reject their fathers' experiences, eager to create their own.

As a way of relating the parents' adolescent decade with the adolescent's own decade, the therapist can pose thoughtful questions such as, "At what age do you believe you had the most fun? What did you do? How do you think your parents had fun when they were your age? What are some of the difficulties teenagers face? Do you think it is easier or more difficult to grow up today than when your parents grew up? Why? How do you think it will be for your own children in the next decade? How can you prepare for the next decade?"

The ideas for working with adolescents offered in this chapter are only a few of the many that can be generated using lyrics as the springboard. Therapists have found the Paraverbal Communication Method of using lyrics metaphorically to be the most successful manner of establishing communication with adolescents and enabling them to communicate freely and effectively with each other. They become open to discussion because of the relevance of the topics in their own media. By listening to the music, reading the lyrics, and discussing meaningful issues within a comfortable, familiar format, adolescents can effectively communicate what is important to them and learn to move toward more meaningful roles in their world.

10

The Child as "Assistant Therapist"

In an effort to improve the poor educational achievement in the United States, many concerned professionals are actively engaged in research in various areas of child development, both cognitive and social. Interactive strategies that have stirred interest involve peer approaches and peer activities that have become a major focus of research in many educational and therapeutic facilities.

Children helping children is not a new idea. Peer tutoring, for example, when appropriately structured, is effective because of what takes place with the participants. There occurs fundamental pleasurable and meaningful interaction, in which each child is accepted by the other. Empathy with each other develops as the two participants share common situations and difficulties. Reciprocity takes place and the self-esteem of both participants is raised.

177

The child who functions as the "teacher" feels significant imparting his or her knowledge or insight and the "learner" learns from his equal rather than from an authority figure, which may represent unpleasant learning experiences. There is then an opportunity for the roles to change. The "learner" now becomes the "teacher" and can share his area of strength with his peer now in the learner role.

The value of the peer interactive approach, that is, of children helping children to develop appropriately was recognized several years ago and utilized in Paraverbal Communication at two prominent mental health facilities. Structuring peers to interact and assist each other occurred as a normal consequence of the Paraverbal Communication Method because of the nature of the approach. In Paraverbal Communication sessions, children engage in pleasurable maneuvers, such as producing rhythmic patterns on percussion instruments, dramatizing feelings, and utilizing novel sensorimotor materials in unique ways. Variations of the use of these materials develop spontaneously by the children during the sessions with the support of the therapist.

Children obtain pleasure from having the therapist or another child interact with him or copy his created sounds or movements. Therefore, the staff thought that Paraverbal Communication was the ideal therapeutic environment for reaching unreachable children with specific but different needs. This child–child interactive approach was the initial step in having a child function as "assistant therapist" in Paraverbal Communication where children could work as peers to benefit each other. The cases further on in the chapter will illustrate how individual children in these facilities functioned as "assistant therapists" in Paraverbal Communication.

Learning by teaching is a central concept to which Paraverbal Communication readily lends itself. A child acting as "assistant therapist" and his peer learner can feel empowered as they make choices and take appropriate responsibility for their actions in the sessions. The children are no longer estranged and alienated because they are active participants and pleasurably involved. Children participating in a session involving an "assistant therapist" learn to relate to each other and to individuals outside the sessions. Specific maneuvers are used according to the children's needs of the moment and can be initiated by "assistant," peer, or therapist as the situation demands.

Specific maneuvers, Paraverbal techniques, and rationale used in the "assistant therapist" or peer interactive approach were described in Chapter 3.

Case 1—A and T

Three illustrations of child as "assistant therapist" are described below, the first one of a 13-year-old girl, A, who worked with a 4-year-old girl, T. This case, with its positive results, formed the foundation for constructive peer work with many other uninvolved resistant children. The older child was given the title of "Assistant Therapist" as she jointly interacted to involve and help the inaccessible younger child.

Paraverbal Communication was used to facilitate the treatment of A, who was suffering from ulcerative colitis and whose lack of trust rendered her unable to relate to others or to benefit from traditional psychotherapy. However, A was able to make constructive use of the many varied channels of communication offered her by Paraverbal Communication. Therefore, these sessions were considered an optimal environment in which to gain trust by helping a peer. A, like other children selected to be the "assistant therapist," was quick to understand how the flexible maneuvers were designed to help their patient. The variety and simplicity inherent in the maneuvers of Paraverbal Communication made it possible to reach and therapeutically benefit A. The alli-

ance with the therapist gave her a needed sense of significance. At the same time, the nurturing regressive work she
had to employ in helping to treat the younger child automatically resulted in her using the same maneuvers so that she
could at the same time satisfy her own childish needs with
dignity. A often spontaneously used the therapeutic situation to project many of her own problems onto her "patient."
As the therapist and A as her assistant strove together to
treat the younger child, her trust in the therapist developed
because she was able to observe the therapist's accepting
and interested attitude toward both the younger child and
herself.

The outcome of this case was remarkably successful. A
became able to cope with her hidden anger toward her parents and her brother as well as with her sense of inadequacy
in school and at home. Once her relationship with the therapist became established, she was able to accept confrontation with resulting surcease from her presenting illness. Her
deep satisfaction in the communicative improvement in her
young patient added to her sense of achievement.

Case 2—T and W

T, the "assistant therapist" was a 9-year-old boy whose
diagnosis on admission to a leading psychiatric facility was
conduct disorder and prepubertal depression, manifested in
poor self-control and continued fighting with peers. He also
suffered from separation anxiety and lack of concentration.
He was put on 145-mg imipramine three times per day.
When the depressive symptoms lifted after 6 weeks, the
medication was discontinued. Then his provocative, aggressive, and uncontrollable behavior came to the fore. Since he
had poor ability to concentrate and could not be engaged in
any of the traditional forms of therapy, it was decided that a
different technique be tried. Asked whether he would be

willing to help the therapist in working with W, an elective mute girl on the ward, he was pleased and eager to begin. With the new peer treatment method in mind, the immediate goals for T were to develop appropriate communicative behavior, to give him a sense of competence and mastery, to develop his trust, to develop his ability to relate to people, and to improve his impulse control, all of which he needed to help him develop in both behavioral and cognitive areas.

W, the peer with whom T was to work as "assistant therapist," was a 9-year-old girl who was brought to the hospital because of depression and elective mutism. When interviewed, she displayed very shallow affect, looked depressed, and would answer only occasionally by whispering one word or nodding her head. She remained rigidly in one position throughout the interview. Although she talked to her family freely, at school she communicated with her teacher and fellow students only by using a toy telephone. Although some of the immediate goals for W were similar to those of her peer, the "assistant therapist," her needs differed in two respects: W needed to develop her verbal communication and she did not need to deal with impulse control. The following two sessions were extrapolated from the total of 16 sessions.

Session 1

On entering the room T and W were offered a choice of percussion instruments. T chose the large conga drum with which he had to demonstrate twice before W would participate in its use. When she finally did, the therapist moved the session ahead by introducing a pair of cymbals to stimulate metaphoric communication of feelings. Again, W needed T's encouragement and example before making a timid attempt to follow his lead and use the cymbals to show her own feelings, which were feelings of sadness.

At this point it seemed strategic for the therapist to in-

troduce a folk song whose lyrics could be used metaphorically to stimulate communication of feelings. This
technique is described in Chapter 9. With these two children, the therapist adapted the technique by using lyrics
that permitted children to insert and substitute concrete
words that had to do with their own feelings. For example,
in the song, "Kumbaya," there are the following lines:
"Someone's singing," "Someone's walking," and so forth.
The children substituted their feelings and sang, "Someone's
happy," "Someone's sad," "Someone's crying." T chose the
word "happy." When he asked W to choose a word, she replied, softly, "crying." He showed great interest and asked,
"What about?" W answered softly, "If someone went on a
trip and left you alone." It was her first whole phrase.

Following this, the therapist introduced a song for the
peers that encouraged imitation of movements expressing affect. T produced an angry movement and was delighted
when W spontaneously identified it. Then, in order to stimulate more verbalization about his anger, the therapist asked
T, "Angry at what?" and he quickly replied, "Angry at my
mother when she don't come to see me when she promises."
The therapist then asked, "What do you do?" and T said, "I
hit the kids around me cause they tease me that my mother
don't come." W was fascinated by what he said. The therapist said to him that she thought talking might be a better
way of handling his anger and asked if he could think of
something to say that would make him feel better and yet
not get him into trouble. W was most interested and leaned
forward. T expressed reluctance to tell the therapist what he
would say, but she assured him that all communication was
acceptable in the therapy room. She suggested that he make
the motion again to show what he had on his mind and then
to say what he was thinking and feeling. "OK" he said, and
yelled, "Shit."

W's eyes opened wide and she stood quite still at his
dramatic behavior. T noticed her interest and urged her to

imitate him, which she did, although not to his satisfaction. He said, "That's not hard enough." She then followed his suggestion and thrust out both hands in an angry hitting motion. T was delighted and said to her, "Now go ahead and say it." She looked at him, then at the therapist, who encouraged her by saying, "It's OK, say it out loud. Lots of children do." With that, W loudly imitated T when he shouted "shit" again. Then she giggled.

Not to let the session get out of hand, the therapist gave each child colored chalk and a large piece of construction paper. She encouraged them to select the colors they wanted and to chalk to the music when she gave them the signal to begin. W's chalking was in light, short strokes, T's were large and colorful. The children spontaneously compared their chalking and admired each others' product. They had learned how to respond to structure. They had learned how to communicate with each other and with the therapist. Both looked more at ease than when they had begun the session.

Session 10

The 10th session illustrated T's increasingly appropriate and confident behavior as he took pride and pleasure in helping W overcome her rigidity and silence. T started by tapping out a rhythmic pattern and asked W to guess the kind of feeling he was expressing, the carryover from the previous session where there had been so much communication of affect. W replied that it sounded scary. The children's interchange led to their speaking of what made them angry. The therapist then introduced a paraphrase of a song to help them further ventilate their feelings. The song was "Shoo Fly Don't Bother Me" but the therapist told them they could substitute any word they wanted or any person they wanted not to bother them, as it says in the song. W immediately said, "Grandpa, don't bother me," which prompted T to say he wanted to do one called, "Mama, don't bother me." The therapist carried this communication of feelings still further into another area, which had to do with impulse control. She suggested that T sing, "Mama" and that W answer with the phrase, "Don't bother me." Both W and T displayed great pleasure in this peer dialogue.

Results

Both children showed progress through the use of the peer interaction technique, which is part of the "assistant therapist" method. T showed great impulse control on the ward and in the classroom. His acting out disappeared. His teacher said he interacted well with his peers and could take frustration without resorting to violence. He remained a day patient until the end of the term, when he was discharged and sent home. W was also discharged. Her mother reported that her school reports showed that she talked more to peers and adults.

Case 3—J and S

In this case, a Paraverbal Communication student was the therapist. She used as "assistant," a 12-year-old boy J, who had a long history of uncontrolled, aggressive behavior directed primarily against his younger brother. When J was nine, his father, reputedly an alcoholic, committed suicide. J was told that his father had died from a heart attack. It was presumed that children on the street told him the truth. He did not discuss this fact either at home or in the hospital until he became involved with Paraverbal Communication. Since his father's death, J's behavior had been so bizarre that he was placed in a children's residence. After his release, he started to smoke marijuana, drink, and steal. Unable to control him, his mother had him hospitalized. J did not re-

spond adequately to individual, group, or milieu psychotherapy in the hospital. However, in individual Paraverbal
Communication with the therapist, J talked of his father, of
his wish to be like him, and his wish that he had been a
better son. In contrast, on the ward, he continued to be destructive, especially toward S, a 5-year-old schizophrenic
boy, who possibly because he was so far removed from reality, did not fear J. S too had been in one-to-one Paraverbal
Therapy with the same therapist, but had responded only
minimally.

On supervising the work of the therapist with these
children, it occurred to the senior therapist that perhaps J's
energies could be harnessed to help both himself and S by
using the peer or "assistant therapist" technique. The therapist spoke individually to both boys. S was perfectly amen-
able. When she asked J whether he would like to work with
her in helping S grow up and be able to learn and play like
other children, explaining that S's mother was ill and he had
no father, J's interest and compassion were aroused. He immediately identified with S and said, "You mean he has no
father, just like me?" The therapist said, "Yes, he died when
S was a little boy." J suddenly got excited and asked how he
could help. The therapist told him, whereupon he gave the
first piece of historical information that his role as "assistant
therapist" induced: "This will be good. It won't be like
home. Every time I wanted to show my little brother something, my stinking big brother would say, 'shove over, dope,
he's smarter than you.'"

The therapist had a conversation with J after the fourth
session, when S had already left the room. She asked, "Can
you tell me why S responds to you so well? He talks to you,
he is able to say what he wants to do and even create new
ways of doing things. He has lost his echo style of speaking
altogether. He looks much more at peace and so much more
happy since he's been working with you. What do you think
it is that you do that a grown person like me is not able to

do?" Without hesitation, J said, "You see, with you, child-hood is already gone a long time and you really don't know what he feels and what he wants. But I'm closer to him in age and that's why he listens to me and enjoys being with me." It was good insight into the function of the peer or "assistant therapist" approach.

J's experience as "assistant therapist" during his work with his peer helped him in the following ways: (1) he was no longer aggressive and abusive toward S, (2) he became interested in S's welfare, development, and pleasure, (3) he himself had pleasure in his new relationship with S through being a model for him. He also enjoyed the dignity of being the "assistant," (4) his uncontrolled energy as well as his dramatic talents were harnessed in a new way—to help someone else, and (5) his self-concept was vastly improved, so that, instead of feeling like the "bad" son, he now felt that he was good and useful.

Summary

As demonstrated, children can learn appropriate cognitive and social behavior and teach it to other children through Paraverbal Communication. By employing peer or "assistant therapist" intervention, a school or ward can become a place where interesting learning and developments can occur, where students are turned on, not off, and where there can be a leap in development.

11

Mother and Child Learn to Communicate through Paraverbal Maneuvers

A mother and a child who can communicate effectively develop a relationship through which the child can develop in positive ways. The communication begins as the newborn reacts to the new environment, primarily to the caretaker–mother and she in turn responds sensitively to the infant. The quality of her response to the infant's rhythms, signals, pacing, and preferences can set in motion a chain of mother–child sharing interactions that can contribute greatly to the child's subsequent development.

As a result of many socioeconomic changes in our lives today, increasing numbers of working mothers spend whole days away from their infants and growing children. This reduced time for interactive development between mother and child makes even more urgent the ability to communicate meaningfully during the time mother and child are together.

189

A growing population, that of adolescent mothers, is producing a large number of young children similarly lacking the kind of care needed for appropriate emotional and cognitive development. Many of these teenage mothers have not themselves fully developed emotionally and generally have their own unmet needs for nurture. They are therefore unable to adequately meet their children's needs for nurture and care.

What does an infant need from the mother? Food, caregiving, protection, and appropriate stimulation, so as to instill an early sense of trust and attachment. Erikson (1980) speaks of "early infant–mother communication as a mutual synchrony and adjustment of interactions between the two such that the interaction creates a sense of trust. Early communication patterns... eventuate in secure patterns of expectation and faith in each other's signals and supports." Thus fortified, the infant develops into a young child ready to cautiously move away from mother, explore the world, and learn. The child does this by observing, reacting, and participating in social, affective, and sensorimotor experiences. Through these active processes, the child develops in two significant ways: (1) he gains confidence in his own abilities, and (2) he begins to perceive himself as separate from his mother. That the many successful mother–child interactions strengthen the child's capacity for positive development is attested to by Cohen (1976). "Each communicative behavior represents an extension of previous use, achieving a more functional and adaptive role over time."

If early communication is not established, a chain of mother–child interactions ensue that may result in behavioral difficulties in the young child and mothering difficulties in the mother. Ainsworth (1977), among many other researchers, reports on the importance of early mother–infant patterns in establishing later infant responses. "It appears that by the second quarter (of the first year), a vicious spiral has built up, so that maternal ineptness and negative infant responses are reciprocally related from then on."

"In any treatment center for children in prelatency, there is a steady flow of children who are neither neurotic nor psychotic, but who show striking disturbances in developmental balance and progression. What these children seem to need therapeutically is a *second* infancy, a chance to repeat and relive the developmental process around a corrective identification" (Alpert 1957).

Paraverbal Communication has been successfully used to interrupt that vicious negative spiral and help establish effective communication between mothers and children, allowing children to relive an improved developmental process. Communication takes place because mostly sensorimotor interactions are structured to elicit responses from both mother and child (rhythmic tapping and pulling, initiating and imitating each other's movements). Therefore, neither mother nor child's behavioral or verbal offerings are ignored; rather, they are specifically responded to through reciprocal and synchronous interactions on the part of mother, child, and therapist. The Paraverbal maneuvers employ the very kinds of materials that foster this kind of reciprocal and synchronous mother–child interaction that is sorely missing in the relationship. The sensorimotor maneuvers used are specifically geared to the primary learning modalities of the young child, the playing–nurturing repertoire of the mother, and the development of attachment between mother and child. Simple, easy-to-use elastic rope, sponge nerf balls, soap bubbles, bells, percussion instruments, and similar child-oriented materials are used in an atmosphere of pleasure. The Paraverbal maneuvers can (1) restructure the mother's existing communicative strategies that may not be effective and (2) teach new strategies and create an awareness of the importance of communication in the child's development. Through the Paraverbal experiences that elicit positive responses from her child, the mother can become aware of the importance of communication in her child's behavioral and cognitive development.

The therapist encourages, accents, and elaborates upon the mother and child's own rhythmic patterns, vocalizations, movements, and dramatizations. She quickly substitutes one medium for another to maintain attention and provide the pleasure that accompanies novelty. Using her voice, face, gestures, and body movement, the therapist also becomes a model for expressive and communicative behavior.

The child acquires a greater awareness of his body's capabilities as well as a sense of mastery through the use of drums, nerf-like balls, and other interactional materials. In reciprocal interactions like imitative tapping or mime, he also learns to wait his turn. The mother, too, learns to wait for her child's response before continuing her own actions (Stern [1974] discussed the importance of this timing sensitivity in mother–infant interaction.) As they participate in reciprocal actions and respond to each other, the child learns what to expect and the mother learns to appropriately nurture, manage, and take pleasure in her child. As the therapist often improvises lyrics to describe the interactions taking place, the child can begin to link actions and words. Through reciprocal dramatization and discussion of feelings, a child begins to link words to feelings, thereby helping him to communicate.

The following two examples illustrate how Paraverbal Communication was utilized to develop mother–child communication; the first involves C, an adolescent single parent who learns how to manage her oppositional toddler son J. The second example illustrates how 8-year-old D and her mother P learn to interact appropriately and assume their natural roles of daughter nurtured by mother rather than daughter nurturing mother, a situation that can occur in this type of distorted dyad. Stern (1974) points out how crucial for healthy development are sensitivity, empathy, flexibility, and creativity in mother–infant interactions. Although C and P each had a different experience with their infants, both now engage in disturbed mother–child interactions. In these two cases, both mothers and children were in need of recognition and pleasure. C and P needed to learn appropriate ways of interacting with their children. C needed to interact with her son in a nurturing manner so as to elicit from him positive responses rather than oppositional behavior. She then could reciprocate and continue the healthy interactive cycle. P did not take care of her infant daughter until age 3; she also needed to nurture her child. As D and her mother P had missed crucial bonding and subsequent appropriate interaction, D was starved for nurture from her mother. In her attempt to obtain this nurture she took on inappropriate responsibilities, thereby neglecting her own development and sense of identity. Therefore, an urgent objective in the Paraverbal sessions was to enable P to recognize her daughter's own unique identity and need for nurture. Only in this way could she begin to interact with D in ways conducive to her development.

Both mothers lacked early nurture and, as a result, were unable to provide for their children what they themselves had not received. Through the specific goal-directed use of pleasurable maneuvers, both mothers gained the needed appropriate nurture, experienced increased self-esteem through their own accomplishments in using Paraverbal Communication, and, in turn, developed pride in their children for their achievements.

Case 1—C and J

C, who was a 16-year-old single parent, sought assistance in an out-patient clinic with the management of her 3½-year-old son J. C also had an 8-month-old daughter. The father was not involved with the family. C reported that J was "hyperactive and did not listen to her." She stated that at times J was very affectionate with her and that she did not understand why at other times he did not listen to her. C stated that J did not speak much English, because she spoke mostly Spanish to him at home. J loved to play but did not get along well with other children. C wanted to send J to a nursery program but worried that J would have problems because of his behavior. The Clinical Team suggested that J and his mother be offered Paraverbal Communication to develop appropriate mother–child interactive skills and communication. With ability to communicate and interact appropriately, J would then be able to more effectively benefit from nursery school and have the opportunity for positive development.

C and J participated in nine Paraverbal Communication sessions. As the sessions progressed, C became increasingly more able to provide appropriate nurture and structure for J. He, in turn, responded to her appropriate behavior through the stimulus of the sound and movement maneuvers and began to exercise impulse control. He eagerly attended to the maneuvers, and as C noted, "does not act hyperactive."

The specific maneuvers that were utilized in the sessions and the effects the interactions had on J and his mother are described below. The reason(s) for using particular materials or introducing a specific maneuver at a particular time will generally be found in parentheses following the maneuver. Purposeful goal-directed interactions are employed in the Paraverbal sessions, and it is of the essence that professionals fully understand the reasons for choosing from the rich armamentarium of materials. Therefore, special emphasis is placed on pointing out the purposes of the maneuvers. Otherwise, the Paraverbal maneuvers become mere early childhood games or pastimes.

It is important to emphasize that contributing to C's inability to nurture J was her own lack of nurture. Nurture was unavailable to J because of her own unmet needs. She stated that she was one of nine children and "it was hard." As sessions progressed, C spontaneously commented on the fun she was having and she recalled and initiated variations of games and songs she had liked as a child. (C was able to therapeutically regress through appropriate sound and movement maneuvers.) Through the pleasurable Paraverbal interactional maneuvers, her own nurture needs were addressed. In the process, she began to learn through concrete mother–child interactions, how to nurture J, and significantly, how to avoid dysfunctional interaction with her 8-month-old daughter. In short, C learned how to be a more effective mother.

The initial goals were to provide both J and C with structured synchronous and reciprocal nurturing interactions in which they had pleasure. Longer term goals were to develop communication and attachment between C and J and to foster age-appropriate behavior in the mother and her children. Another significant goal was to help J and C with the separation–individuation task and enable J to develop a healthy sense of separateness (Mahler 1972). A third goal was to help develop J's (English) language.

Session 1

J, C, and the baby came to the first session. After all were seated comfortably, the therapist handed a set of wrist bells to J and one to C. She gently pulled J's bells and began to chant, "Pull-ing, pull-ing, back and forth," while rocking rhythmically sideways. (The therapist's goal was to encourage pleasure in kinesthetic stimulation and the feeling of safety and trust that can be attained from synchronous, rhythmic body movement.) To encourage mother–child interaction, the therapist then changed words to, "Mommy pulls, J pulls, Mommy pulls, J pulls," and waited for each to do his part. J, stimulated by the words, smiled and looked at his mother. (To maintain J's interest, further stimulate him, and to reinforce their pleasure, the therapist varied the tempo and dynamics of the maneuver and joined them for support.) She told them that this time they would pull slowly, then fast, and chanted, "We pull slowly, we pull slowly," accompanied by slow movements, and then, "we pull fast, we pull fast," accompanied by fast movements. J and C laughed as they enjoyed the novel synchronous experience. When the bells slipped from J's wrist, mother told him to hold tight ("duro") and helped him secure them. The therapist encouraged C's assistance with J, and said, "Now, you and Mommy pull slow and then fast just like we all did together," and improvised chanting while C and J rocked synchronously and pleasurably. "Pulling, pulling back and forth... now we pull slow-ly, we pull slow-ly... now we pull fast, we pull fast... Mommy pulls J, J pulls Mommy, back and forth, back and forth." C and J laughed, delighted with the stimulation of the movement and each other. (The structure, rhythmic pulling back and forth, was also designed to promote J's impulse control and to harness his hyperactivity. In addition, the improvised descriptive words developed his language.) The therapist suggested other variations using the bells that linked them together to enable J and his mother to continue their pleasure and also to begin to introduce new words for J to learn. They all stood and she chanted, "Now we swing up, now we swing down" as they followed the cues. C knelt in front of J to enable them to swing together. (J experienced the directional movement accompanied by chanting of the words up and down, back and forth, and slow and fast. The experience of his active participation helped develop his language ability, while the tactile experience itself provided nurture for both C and J.) Then, the therapist added another movement experience, "crossing, cross-ing," and C and J swung their arms across their bodies in a playful manner. The therapist praised C for the skillful manner in which she worked with her son and J for his own efforts. C smiled at the recognition.

The therapist then introduced the sound of a new instrument, the maracas, to sustain J's attention. She handed one to C and suggested she give it to J (to enable her to begin to provide nurture, pleasure, and leadership for her son). J accepted the maracas and assistance in using them from his mother and then both sang and participated in another improvised song. "Mommy and J shake high, Mommy and J shake low." The therapist suggested to C that she and J exchange instruments ("so J can learn from you") and repeat the song. C asked J to change with her and gave J the bells she had been using. J eagerly handed her the maracas, anticipating the pleasure of the next interaction. The therapist continued the chanting, accompanying on a tambourine, "We shake loud, we shake soft, we shake high, we shake low, we shake together." J watched his mother as she provided cues for him and he imitated her.

To maintain J's attention and to reinforce the intimacy of their interaction, the therapist handed C and J each a small cymbal and invited them to sit so that they all faced each other. (By tapping the cymbals together, the participants produced a new, ringing sound and the seated position further encouraged intimacy.) The therapist demonstrated how she would tap each one, and chanted, "I tap Mommy, I tap J," then gestured for C to tap, "Mommy taps J, Mommy taps me," then the therapist leaned toward J, and chanted "I tap J, J taps me," and then pointed to Mommy and chanted, "J taps Mommy, J taps Mommy." C spontaneously moved toward J, so that he could easily reach her. (C appeared to be learning appropriate helping-nurturing behavior as she modeled the therapist's behavior, and this new learning was apparent as a natural outgrowth of the Paraverbal maneuvers with J in the sessions. The cymbal tapping maneuver provided tactile stimulation, helped J with impulse control, reinforced his separate identity, and provided reciprocal pleasure for both mother and child.)

The therapist introduced another new instrument, the

autoharp, so that they could remain in the intimate seated position. C immediately showed interest in it and spoke about a teacher in her junior high school who played one. (As the autoharp stirred pleasant memories, the therapist encouraged the discussion.) C asked to play it and strummed across the strings while the therapist improvised and sang, "I like Mommy, I like J. Mommy plays the autoharp, J watches Mommy." C smiled at J. He touched the autoharp and the therapist arranged the autoharp between J and his mother so they could play it together. The therapist said, "Do like Mommy" and C strummed. J imitated her. C smiled proudly and said, "Good, J." More improvisations followed: "I like J, I like Mommy, I like sister, Mommy and J make music." (By putting C's and J's actions into words, the therapist provided structure for mother and child to interact appropriately and for J to learn language.)

In order for C and J to have another gratifying mother–child imitation experience, the therapist introduced a song of imitation, "Whatever I Do, Do Like Me" and made simple movements for them to copy. C spoke in Spanish to J, telling and showing him how to copy the movements. Synchronously, they imitated clapping, raising their hands up, and tapping their knees. To enable C to become the model for her son, the therapist changed the words to "Whatever Mommy does, we'll do like Mommy." C patted her cheeks, then patted herself on the head. The therapist and J copied her and C looked pleased at being imitated. Then the therapist chanted and pointed to J, "Whatever J does, we'll do like J." He patted his head just like he had seen his mother do; C and the therapist both imitated his movements. C encouraged him to make a different movement. He jumped. They all jumped. The therapist nurtured C by telling her that J was quick at learning. She smiled proudly at his ability to learn and for her newly effective management of him. (J giggled with glee at his own sense of power in getting his mother and the therapist to imitate his jumping. His self-confidence was growing and, as a result, he was approaching tasks in a more attentive, focused, and therefore competent manner.)

They all sat on the floor to include the baby. (The floor provided additional safety for the rhythmic and pleasurable interactions that could frequently include the baby. In addition, it was a strategy that helped J with his problem of restlessness as new body positions were taken.) The therapist asked C if she thought the baby would cry if they all sat around her. C said it was all right to do it. J spontaneously moved in closer to them. They joined hands around the baby, rocked sideways and sang, "Row, Row, Row Your Boat." Both J and C rocked pleasurably; C looked happy that the baby was included. As a result of her pleasure, C spontaneously picked up the bells, shook them gently at the baby, and was delighted when the baby reached for them. They joined hands around the baby again and sang, "Ring around the baby, she is nice, J is nice, Mommy is nice." The therapist commented on how well J moved his body. Again, C smiled proudly.

The therapist stood for the session's final maneuver. She handed J and C wrist bells to recall and reinforce the pleasant interaction they had experienced in the initial pulling maneuver. She chanted, "We are swinging, we are swinging, we swing up, we swing down" and everyone swung their linked hands up and down. J laughed as he was gently swung into the air. He wanted to do it again. The therapist told him to chant with the motions, "Up" and then "Down." He laughed as he sang "Up" as he swung up, and the same for "Down," experiencing pleasure as he reinforced his expanding language.

J then asked to play with a car. He had learned quickly that it was safe to ask to use materials in the sessions. C added that he liked cars and always played with them at home. The therapist said she didn't have one, but they could pretend. This was a good opportunity to demonstrate to C how she could learn to improvise to meet her son's needs. The therapist handed J and C a tambourine with its jangling sound to use as a steering wheel and dramatized, "Drive, drive, drive the car, we drive slow, we drive fast." They both imitated the therapist's movements of driving and then J responded to the structure of the maneuver and marched across the room rhythmically (rather than run about in an out of control manner). The therapist and C were caught up in his rhythmic driving and accompanied him, "Drive, drive, drive the car." At the end of session, C said she had fun and said she knew J did too.

In presenting sensorimotor stimulation through the Paraverbal materials and maneuvers in this first session, the therapist encouraged active exploration and improvisation, nurturing-leadership opportunities for C, and learning and pleasure for both. A primary objective of the initial sessions was for trust to begin to develop as J experienced repetition of pleasurable interactions with his mother. The therapist encouraged appropriate sensorimotor movement and accompanying language. As J participated independently of his mother, as well as with her, his own autonomy and separation from her were reinforced, his sense of competence strengthened as he experienced his own impact on her, and age-appropriate language could be learned. The Paraverbal maneuvers provided a variety of sensorimotor experiences for J to be exposed to age-appropriate preoperational Piagetian concepts. Furthermore, through the active reciprocal experiences, J began to have reinforced the "holding versus letting go" developmental objectives that Erikson believes so crucial to trust.

Session 2

In the second session, the therapist built upon the first session's interactions and incorporated variations of maneuvers that J and his mother had enjoyed. C told the therapist that J liked the song, "Row, Row, Row Your Boat," which he had learned the previous week. She said he asked her to sing it at home and they sang and rocked together. C also said that J liked dramatizing the words "up" and "down" and so the therapist handed wrist bells to them and all three repeated this synchronous maneuver holding onto the bells.

The therapist offered J a choice of different sized balls to provide more pleasure and encourage him to begin to make appropriate choices. He reached for a large ball and when encouraged to roll it to the therapist, he did. She chanted, "I roll the ball to J, J rolls the ball to me." Then, "I roll the ball to Mommy, Mommy rolls the ball to J, J rolls the ball to Mommy." They continued the rhythmic rolling movement and joined the therapist in chanting. (The structure of the words and rhythmic movement maintained J's attention and enabled him to focus on his actions; he thereby achieved a sense of mastery and his self-esteem was strengthened.)

J pointed to the autoharp that they had used in the previous session. C supported J's nonverbal request for the autoharp and said, "He loves to play that thing." (C appeared to be identifying with J because she too wanted to play it.) The therapist placed the autoharp between them so that they could take turns. J spontaneously strummed across the strings and C pressed the chord buttons to accommodate him. The therapist chanted, "Mommy and J play together." Then the therapist strummed across the strings hard and immediately silenced them by placing her hands across them. C and J laughed. Then C, imitating the therapist, strummed hard and silenced the strings. Again, she laughed pleasurably. Wanting to share her pleasure, C took J's hand and with hers over it, strummed hard and then placed his tiny hands across the strings to silence them. Both laughed and C praised her son. "Good J." After this happy interaction, the therapist then introduced a song for C so that she too could experience nurture. The therapist asked her if she knew the song, "Kumbaya;" she said she did. After singing the words, "Someone's singing, Kum-baya," the therapist asked C what else "someone" might be feeling that they could sing about, and C said, "Someone's happy." They sang it together, with C taking the lead.

At this time, the therapist introduced a new sound from a small percussion instrument to further develop the mother–child interaction. The therapist handed the castanets to C and suggested that she give one to J. (With each new maneuver, the therapist's objective was to encourage the mother to provide the new experience for the child and thereby represent pleasure, begin to initiate appropriate nurturing interactions, and establish the mother's leadership.) The therapist demonstrated how to tap a verbal message by clicking the castanets together to accompany the words, "Hel-lo J, hel-lo Mom-my." C spontaneously imitated the therapist and then rhythmically clicked the castanets and said, "Hel-lo J, I love you J." J immediately said, "I love you, Mommy." C was reminded that J always hugged her and was affectionate when she tended to the baby. The therapist let her know how important this information was as it was J's way of saying, "love me too" and that he still required nurturing attention. She explained that this kind of intimate playful interaction with J could show him that she cared for him all of the time.

J spontaneously picked up and tapped the tambourine that was nearby. (His attention was captured and maintained by the various sounds of the particular materials the therapist had provided for that session.) She and C picked up small drums and imitated J. He smiled at this immediate approval. (The materials also permitted him to ventilate appropriately rather than randomly acting out and he experienced the needed sense of mastery.) J then reached for his mother's drum. She responded by exchanging drums with him. The therapist commented to C that J wanted to be like her and that by responding to him as she did, she was helping him to learn how to behave. Then, to reinforce her position of maternal leadership with J, the therapist told C to demonstrate a pattern on the drum for him. She tapped lightly with her nails and J copied her. C looked gratified and tapped another pattern with her knuckles and he again copied her. She then initiated a pattern with the heel of her hand. J did the same. (All of these patterns, initiated by C, and copied by J, have provided for him a sense of competence, and he began to substitute pleasurable, structured movement for hyperactive behavior. The structure inherent in the pleasure-producing maneuvers was instructive for C. It has enabled her to relate appropriately to J.)

The therapist introduced rope pulling for the final maneuver. (This rocking maneuver which had brought them together at the beginning of the session reinforced their sense of synchronous interaction, feelings of safety, and pleasure. The structure of the maneuver kept them focused and thus able to achieve the spontaneous pleasure that otherwise might not have been possible.) Each one held a section of the elastic rope as the therapist chanted, "Pull-ling, pull-ling, back and forth, pull-ing, pull-ing, back and forth." C asked to pull it fast and said, "rapido" to J. (C is beginning to anticipate and prepare J.) J squealed with delight and held tight. (The Paraverbal maneuvers that provide nurturing interactions for participants of any age fostered in C free communication and expression of her own pleasure–nurture needs.) In response to C's request, the therapist alerted them that this time she would pull "rapido–fast" and then chanted, "Now, we'll pull fast, now we'll pull fast, J pulls fast, Mommy pulls fast." C and J, caught up in the stimulating interaction, chanted, laughed freely, and then hugged each other.

This second session was structured to accomplish a number of goals: (1) to continue to provide pleasure, (2) to introduce J to the concept of making choices and thereby reinforce his sense of identity, (3) to provide opportunities for C to take on more maternal leadership, set appropriate

limits for J, and provide pleasure for him, (4) to provide opportunities for C to receive nurture and have fun as she recalled pleasureful experiences from her own childhood, and
(5) to enable C to receive praise for her appropriate nurturing of J. New materials were introduced for mother–child interactions and there were many opportunities for
spontaneity and freedom of choice of maneuver or material.
Both C and J felt pleasure in this freedom and spontaneously
initiated interactions accordingly. Both ventilated feelings
using sound and movement. C communicated her happy
feelings through the metaphoric use of lyrics, and given the
opportunity for reciprocal cymbal tapping in an intimate interaction, J and his mother communicated their mutual love
for each other. They exercised their choices of small and
large body movements for appropriate release of tension.
The flexibility of the Paraverbal maneuvers to provide means
of communication at the needed moments could be seen at
work for C and J as each was stimulated and felt free to initiate therapeutic interactions. The self-images of both J and C
were raised as their actions were imitated and reciprocated
and they were praised for their appropriate interaction. Finally, C gained significant insight through the maneuvers
about her own feelings and how they related to J and the
baby. With the new insight, she began to behave more appropriately with her children. The Paraverbal sessions provided repeated optimal practicing opportunities for her. J
and C were making effective progress.

Session 3

In the third session, the therapist introduced the chalking to music maneuver to enable J and C to share another
kinesthetic experience and to provide an opportunity for J to
observe his mother's movements. The maneuver introduced
new stimuli—color, rhythmic sound, and a standing position where greater freedom of movement prevailed. The

chalking maneuver was another of the many Paraverbal communicative opportunities that reinforced pleasurable interactions between mother and child. The therapist placed them on opposite sides of an easel that held large black construction paper. Large pieces of colorful chalk were stacked nearby. Stimulated by the rhythm of "March Militaire," C moved her arms freely and made circular motions all over the paper. J, after pressing hard on his chalk and making vertical lines, joined his mother on her side as she chalked pleasurably. She moved closer to J, handed him a piece of chalk, and invited him to chalk with her on her paper. He made small chalk marks at the bottom and watched her as she made colorful rhythmic markings all over the paper, creating a colorful nonobjective free-flowing chalking. J tried to imitate her movements and C nodded her head in approval. After the maneuver ended, C said that she liked doing this and would like to do it at home with J. (The maneuver provided a sense of mastery and pleasure for both J and C. J enjoyed being close to his mother, having pleasure with her, and creating his own unique product. C experienced pleasure from the absolute freedom of movement, having her son imitate her movements, and producing her own unique colorful creation.)

The therapist introduced a new maneuver, still involving sound, this time with C's favorite, the autoharp. (to continue C's pleasure). The therapist placed a drum in J's lap to involve him and demonstrated how he could tap it to accompany their singing. She strummed and chanted, "I'm on my way," and invited C to echo her words. C repeated, "I'm on my way." J tapped and also tried to repeat the words. In response to where would be the best place to go, C said, "Florida, Disneyworld, and I'd take J with me and we'd go on rides and have fun." J smiled and joyfully repeated, "Disneyworld." (C was able to share with the therapist her fantasy and gratified her need to "get away." She felt safe in revealing this fantasy through the metaphoric use of lyrics

and was able to think about having fun with J outside of the
Paraverbal sessions. She had experienced many gratifying
and pleasurable interactions with J using the Paraverbal materials and could now begin to generalize her new nurturing
behavior. Through their shared pleasure, C and J were able
to be mutually nurturing.)

To reinforce their delight in each other, the therapist introduced a final maneuver designed to provide ventilation,
additional pleasure, and permit C to maintain her modeling
leadership role with her son. The therapist produced soap
bubbles and invited J to break the bubbles that Mommy blew
by clapping them between his hands. (This was another opportunity for J to discharge anxiety and tension by appropriately breaking something—the bubbles.) He squealed
with laughter each time he clapped a bubble between his
hands. He then gestured that he wanted to blow the bubbles. C pointed out to the therapist his need to change roles
with her, and then gave him the wand while she held the
bottle. (C has gained significant insight into her son through
the interaction structured by the maneuvers, and she is beginning to appropriately anticipate his needs.) She used her
imagination freely and with a castanet, burst the bubbles after first allowing J to enjoy watching each one float in the air.

Session 4

In the fourth session, the therapist again introduced J's
and C's favorite and familiar maneuvers, this time to provide
opportunities for C to increase her nurturing leadership role
with J. The structure of the maneuvers and the pleasure J
obtained from them maintained his attention and appropriate play behavior with his mother.

The therapist also continued to introduce new materials. To enable J to experience large body movements and
accompany them with language, the therapist introduced a
hoop through which to climb. When C saw it, she sponta-

neously announced, "I used to play with those things when I was a kid" and playfully circled her waist with the hoop to balance it. (She again recalled her childhood pleasure, but now included her son as she relived it.) J gleefully watched her and then joined her inside the circle. The therapist structured the interaction so that both could participate, but with C taking the lead. The therapist invited C to chant with her, "In and out of the ring, J goes in and out of the ring." (J also chanted, thereby further developing language.) After this, J contributed a new movement; he picked up the ball and gently threw it through the hoop while C held it. J then handed the ball to the therapist. She immediately validated his appropriate spontaneous movement by improvising lyrics to accompany his actions. "J hands me the ball, I hand J the ball." Then J and his mother each took a turn holding the hoop while the other tossed the ball. (J has learned to wait for his cue, the word "go" in many maneuvers after "ready, set." C has learned to provide this structure for him, and he responds eagerly and reciprocally, giving her pleasure and satisfaction in her ability to manage her son. J's hyperactive behavior is diminishing as his movements are channeled into goal-oriented learning interactions.) C and J continued the maneuver, this time taking turns rolling the ball through the hoop. C bent down, rolled the ball, and said, "I bowl a lot" and proceeded to tell and show J how to roll the ball like she does when she bowls. J imitated his mother's arm-swinging motion and C nodded in approval. C's pleasure in the actual maneuver was obvious and was intensified by J's imitation of her. She also took great pride in his learning facility.

J and C alternated their requests for specific maneuvers. C now asked to play the autoharp. (Both felt free to choose from the variety of materials because of the permissive, accepting use of the maneuvers, and they utilized them in their own unique fashion.) They had learned through the maneuvers that it was safe to make choices, that whatever they communicated would be validated by the therapist, and that all would participate.) The therapist placed the auto-harp between them and began to chant, "J and Mommy, they make music." Both J and C strummed the strings syn-chronously, while the therapist pressed the chord buttons. J said, "a mano," showing his mother how he played gently with his hand, rather than the strumming stick. C sponta-neously praised him for his original movement. J beamed with his mother's acceptance.

J then motioned for the bubbles. This time in imitation of the therapist, C structured the interaction, first holding the bubbles as J blew and then suggesting ways to break the bubbles. She looked around the room, picked up the hoop and motioned for Jose to blow the bubbles through it. (Through the structure and very crucial flexibility inherent in the maneuvers, C has become free to create and think of new ways to provide pleasure for J and herself.)

C said that she thought that J would like to do chalking to music. (Again, C's memory of pleasure with the maneu-ver inspired her to request it.) The therapist suggested that they begin with chalking the following week as it was time to end this session. C took her time getting ready to leave. J picked up a kaleidoscope, looked into it, and playfully told J what she saw.

C, who requested and received nurture for herself in the Paraverbal sessions, was becoming better able to nurtur-ingly manage J in the sessions and in general care before and after each session. J was responding age-appropriately to his mother's confident nurturing behavior.

Session 5

In this fifth session, C showed growth as she frequently took the initiative in providing leadership for J and was more spontaneous than in previous sessions. C's self-esteem had improved significantly because of her repeated satisfactory

Paraverbal experiences, and as a result, she was able to interact more appropriately and "naturally" with J and the baby.
She frequently smiled proudly and praised J for his competence with the materials and was also beginning to recognize the significance of responding appropriately to the
baby's curiosity.

J, C, and the therapist sat comfortably on the floor with
the baby in the center. (The sessions were structured to enable the baby to be included without being intrusive and to
ensure that J remained the focus of attention. J's behavior
was always validated by his having choice of material and
the opportunity to initiate a sound or movement within the
group.) The therapist began the session by modeling an interaction with the baby that J and C could imitate. She
handed each of them wrist bells, chanted while shaking
them synchronously, and invited them to join her. "Shake,
shake, shake the bells for baby, up, down, high, low, slow,
fast." All participated synchronously and with joy.

The therapist introduced a small scarf for a maneuver in
which each could "hide" under it and then be "found" again
in a play situation. (The maneuver provides basic feelings of
joy, reassurance, and identity to both participants.) First the
therapist "hid" the baby with the scarf and chanted,
"Where, oh where, oh where is baby?" J laughed and gently
pulled off the scarf and squealed, "There she is." He placed
the scarf on his own head, eager to "be found" as the therapist chanted for J. He waited patiently and C assumed the
natural motherly role, pulled the scarf and chanted in a playfully surprised voice, "There he is." J squealed with laughter
and hurriedly placed the scarf on his head again to repeat
the pleasure. Afterward, J stood and placed the scarf on C's
head and waited for the therapist to chant, "Where, oh
where, oh where is Mommy?" J gleefully pulled the scarf
aside and shouted, "There she is." Both laughed and C
proudly patted J on the head and stated excitedly that they
would play this at home. Both mother and child had experi-

enced the pleasure and delight of being found and finding each other. (In addition to providing pure pleasure for both, the hide and find maneuver helped J with two developmental steps: (1) It helped reinforce an internal representation of his mother as he must picture her in his mind while she is hidden, and (2) it contributed to his developing sense of self as a separate being from his mother. J experienced the exhilaration of the peekaboo game that helps the child to separate and individuate (Mahler 1972). This developmental task typically takes place in most children between 10 and 18 months as they begin to master the tasks of separation from the mother and experience increased autonomy. J at 3½ years was now experiencing the reciprocal tasks that contribute to the successful development of separation–individuation. Through the many structured but pleasurable interactions with his mother, J learned impulse control and how to wait his turn to participate reciprocally. The resultant pleasure and sense of mastery have been powerful incentives for him. They have similarly motivated C to interact appropriately with J.)

The therapist observed that J was looking around the room, having had enough of the hiding, and introduced a rhythmic ball-tossing maneuver that he had frequently requested. (The Paraverbal maneuvers make readily available a variety of materials with which to improvise as the need or desire appears. In this way, communication can be initiated by any participant in his or her chosen manner. The therapist can continually assess progress and interact accordingly.) In response to J's nonverbal communication that he desired a change, the therapist introduced a variation of the ball-tossing maneuver to further stimulate interest and produced two hand drums off which a child can bounce a light sponge ball. J accepted one hand drum and waited as the therapist slowly bounced the ball to him accompanied by improvised lyrics. As J bounced the ball back to her, she continued to improvise lyrics. After repeating this a few times, the therapist handed the hand drum to C, who continued what the therapist had begun. She chanted her own improvised lyrics about J and bounced the ball back to him. They then followed the therapist's improvised cues to bounce the ball up and then catch it. J was extremely pleased with his power to bounce the ball into the air and C appropriately praised him. To add more pleasure to the maneuver and strengthen J's impulse control, the therapist further structured J's movements by having him wait to throw the ball until she said "ready, set, go." J readily agreed and anticipated the pleasure of his action by excitedly holding onto the ball in a ready position. On the cue, he tossed the ball into the air. C then spontaneously moved closer in order to repeat the maneuver with him and J responded joyfully.

Session 6

The sixth session objectives were to expand language for J through the interactive maneuvers and increase opportunities for C to use her own newly acquired experiences to initiate interactions. After tapping messages with the small cymbals, "J taps Mommy, Mommy taps J, J taps softly, Mommy taps softly, J taps loudly, Mommy taps loudly," the therapist demonstrated the same technique using the hands to tap the same messages, "J taps Mommy's hands, Mommy taps J's hands." The therapist asked C what else they could do and she snapped her fingers rhythmically and chanted, "Mommy snaps her fingers, J snaps his fingers" and showed him how to make the snapping sound.

C said she had an idea and reached for the hoop. She told J to step into the hoop and after he did this, to step out of the hoop. He followed her instructions and accepted her gentle assistance. C chanted her own improvisation, encouraging J to join her by holding the hoop as he stepped into the hoop and out again. (This experience provided large-motor, impulse control, and language experience.)

At the end of the session, C asked the therapist if she could recommend nursery schools that would be appropriate for J. She said that J was getting along much better with her at home and that she thought he would now enjoy being in nursery school and playing with other children, a basic problem when he first came for Paraverbal Communication sessions. C said that J could attend to tasks for longer periods of time than previously and that she believed that he could now behave appropriately in a class. The therapist told her she would be happy to assist her.

Results

C and J continued for a few more sessions. It was apparent that C was eager to have J begin nursery school, and she recognized that the Paraverbal sessions had helped prepare J for his next developmental step. C was especially pleased with J's language development. When they initially began the Paraverbal sessions, she had stated, "He doesn't know how to say the words in English." However, in the moments of reduced tension through the pleasurable maneuvers, J did learn the words and C was now hopeful that he could continue to learn in school.

Both J and C were able to communicate their needs and found ways to satisfy those needs through the Paraverbal sensorimotor maneuvers. Both were recognized, accepted, and valued. Their resultant self-confidence encouraged increasing participation, which led to positive needed development for both mother and child.

Through the variety of pleasurable maneuvers, J satisfied his unfulfilled need to actively discover and learn through his own appropriate behavior and experiences. His previous hyperactivity was harnessed into focused but spontaneous, gratifying, appropriate behavior that elicited nurturing behavior from his mother. C learned that she is a primary source of pleasure for her son and understands how to utilize her own unique resources. The Paraverbal maneuvers assisted her in liberating these resources that profoundly affected her son. Through C's resultant appropriate interactions with J, he experienced needed nurturing and pleasure. He also discovered the kind of behavior that elicits more nurturing and pleasure from his mother. Therefore, J and his mother appeared to be able to move on in their respective and interactive development. Paraverbal Communication helped establish the natural cycle of mother–child interaction that seemed never to have developed.

Case 2—D and P

D was a delicate looking 8½-year-old third-grade girl, who lived with her married parents and younger brother and sister, aged 2 and 1. She was referred by the Pediatric Clinic of a teaching hospital because of behavior problems, inattentiveness, and poor academic functioning. Although more proficient in Spanish than English, she was reported to have difficulty understanding verbal directions and expressing herself fluently in either language. She was said to have auditory processing and memory problems. Her teacher reported that D also experienced difficulty relating to her classmates. She tends to sit or stand unusually close to other children, and as a result annoyed them and was rejected. Her mother, P, did not know how to deal with D's recent rebellious, stubborn behavior at home. She was described as a restless child who forgot what she was told to do.

D was born prematurely at 7 months, weighed 2 lbs at birth, and remained in an incubator for 3 months. At home, she was cared for primarily by her maternal grandmother because of her mother's own emotional difficulties in dealing with an alcoholic and violent husband. Her mother was not able to provide consistent care for D or her siblings, and, although D appeared extremely needy of nurture for herself, this 8½-year-old child was saddled with the burden of caring for her siblings as well.

Paraverbal Communication was recommended for D and P to develop mother–child communication. It was felt that P needed to learn how to nurture her daughter and interact appropriately with her. Through these structured, goal-directed therapeutic interactions that made communication possible through sensorimotor channels, it was hoped that D would receive needed nurture, have opportunities to ventilate hidden feelings, and learn language and concepts. Her poor self-esteem could thus be strengthened.

Session 1

D and her mother appeared for their first session 45 minutes late. Mother said she was unable to stay for the appointment but would return later for D. This unexpected development frustrated the immediate goal of the first session, which was to begin to foster mother–child interaction. The therapist therefore restructured the session to enable D to receive needed nurture from her. (The variety and flexibility of therapeutic maneuvers made this type of change in session goals possible.) D appeared saddened by her mother's "desertion." As a way of communicating acceptance of D with her sad feelings, the therapist first introduced the autoharp to accompany improvised lyrics about her sadness. (The autoharp is effective in such a situation because it can be used to create a sense of appropriate intimacy as it is shared by the participants. It is placed horizontally, half on the child's lap, half on the therapist's lap, and the two are face to face.) The therapist placed it on their laps as they faced each other, and chanted while strumming, "Someone's sad, Kumbaya, someone's sad, Kumbaya." D began to hum, then sang the lyrics with the therapist. Her smile was a form of nonverbal communication that she felt accepted and the therapist then continued with nurturing lyrics. "Like somebody, yes I do, like somebody, yes I do, and that person is D." D smiled and asked to have the song repeated and this time sang the words with the therapist. (This was a pleasurable experience for D and a first step in developing trust.) D now took the initiative and strummed the autoharp strings while the therapist pressed the chord buttons and continued to improvise lyrics about D. "I like somebody with a red dress on, red dress on, red dress on, and that person is _____ ." D smiled and exclaimed, "me." Then, the therapist continued, "I like somebody with black shoes on, black shoes on, black shoes on, and that person is _____ ." D became increasingly animated as the therapist got to the end of the verse, and at the appropriate moment, D again proudly announced, "me." After they finished this improvised song, D began exploring the string sounds and plucked a string, making it vibrate loudly. The therapist commented on its loud sound and said it sounded like a father sound. D laughed and plucked another string producing a softer sound. She spontaneously named it "Mother" and did the same with two other strings nearby, also soft, and called them Elizabeth and Gilbert. The therapist praised her for her interesting way of showing her family and D smiled. As D had omitted herself from her family constellation, the therapist then asked, "But where's D?" After giving it some thought and exploring the sounds, she plucked a loud string next to the father sound and said, "That's me."

So that D could continue to receive nurture, experience pleasure, and begin to develop a sense of her own identity, the therapist began to offer her choices of materials. When offered a choice of different sized drums, she chose a large conga floor drum and spontaneously tapped a rhythmic pattern. The therapist immediately copied her and D smiled. Eager to have another pleasurable experience, she asked to do it again. The therapist nodded. D tapped a different more complex pattern, and, when therapist copied it, D again smiled. She was nurtured and satisfied with the validation of her actions. The therapist suggested they tap D's pattern together. D nodded, eager to share something, her rhythmic pattern, with the therapist. (The flexibility and inherent structure of each maneuver enabled the therapist to utilize it to address specific needs as they emerged.) D watched the therapist closely so as to tap synchronously with her. This sharing interaction appeared to be a new experience for D and provided her with great pleasure and further nurture. She asked to repeat it with another rhythmic pattern. After this, the therapist suggested that D now imitate her tapping softly, loud, fast, and slow. D nodded and eagerly waited for the therapist to tap her pattern. The therapist then imitated D's soft, loud, fast, and slow variations. (Through the variations of intensity and tempo, as well as synchronous and reciprocal interaction, D was experiencing pleasure and mastery and taking on the roles both of leader and follower.)

D welcomed the next maneuver, one in which both stood and imitated each other. (The change in body position is effective in maintaining focused attention, and the standing position used in this maneuver provides greater freedom of movement through a variety of body movements. This imitating is designed to increase self-esteem and promote a sense of identity because of the improvised personalized lyrics such as "Whatever we do, we'll do like D.") The therapist introduced the song, "Whatever I Do, Do Like Me," and demonstrated for D how to make a movement such as jumping on one foot or clapping the hands together. (The words and accompanying movements provided a kinesthetic experience integrated with language.) D pleasurefully copied and sang the lyrics. She then spontaneously said, "Now, I'll do one," and the therapist nodded encouragingly. D swayed back and forth while she sang, "Whatever I do, do like me." The therapist swayed in imitation, singing with her and then responded, "Whatever D does, I'll do like she does." D looked happy hearing her name as part of the lyrics and repeated her part. They then took turns initiating other movements. Her hunger for age-appropriate play was apparent and she did not want to stop the interacting or the pleasure. Rather, she offered more ideas and variations in the maneuvers. The therapist praised her for her many ideas.

Recognizing D's hidden sadness even in the midst of the apparent pleasure, the therapist introduced a metaphoric song to allow her to ventilate. They synchronously used the autoharp as the therapist sang, "Go Tell Aunt Rhody the Old Gray Goose Is Dead." As the therapist sang the song, D strummed while reflecting on the words. They discussed the meanings of the words in the song such as goslings and mourning, and when the therapist asked why the children were sad, D said, "because their mother is dead and she couldn't buy them things or take care of them."

D's concern about her mother's ability to care for her and her siblings was communicated through the Paraverbal maneuvers. She took the initiative in the maneuvers just as she took the initiative to ensure her siblings and mother were cared for. But she also took the first step toward appropriate, reciprocal interaction. She frequently tried to structure the therapist in the sessions. But rather than being denied this need, the flexibility of the maneuvers provided opportunities for her to satisfy her need to take the lead, and then at other times learn to follow and experience the pleasure of reciprocity. This cooperative interaction can help her learn how to play more successfully with peers, who currently reject her for her inappropriate play.

Session 2

The second session included D and her mother. The objectives were to raise D's self-esteem through pleasurable interaction with her mother and enable her to ventilate feelings. On entering the room, D saw the drums and recognized the one she had used in the last session, the one that had given her so much pleasure. She chose it again. The

therapist encouraged P to choose an instrument. Assisted
by D, P chose the tambourine. The therapist chose a small
drum. D, accustomed to taking responsibility and nurturing
her mother, now took the lead and tapped a pattern. The
therapist imitated her and invited P to interact with her
daughter by imitating D's pattern, which she did. D smiled,
nodding her head at her mother in appreciation of her imitation. P shrugged her shoulders and returned her smile. (It
was apparent by her surprised look that she was not accustomed to having pleasure with her daughter. It was also evident that P relied heavily on D and following D's lead was
natural for her.) To interrupt this pattern, the therapist suggested that Mother tap her own pattern and that D and the
therapist would imitate her. P shook her head as if to say she
could not think of anything. D spoke to her mother in Spanish and demonstrated how to make up a pattern. P smiled
and tapped a short pattern. D beamed in approval of her and
she and the therapist imitated her mother. P seemed pleased
with her competence and the validation that both D and the
therapist had provided. The therapist then suggested they
tap P's pattern different ways, first with their nails, then the
knuckles, the palm, and D suggested they use the fists and
then the elbows. Her mother laughed and playfully followed
her daugher's cues and seemed just like D, needy of pleasurable nurturing interaction. Once P was comfortable with the
tapping and imitating, the therapist suggested they tap
their names, beginning with D. All synchronously tapped
and chanted D, then P, then the therapist's name. They
tapped and chanted the names first softly, then very loudly,
then softly again. Each was pleased to have the opportunity
to choose her own way to tap her name and be imitated.
(Through this maneuver, repeated but varied pleasurable reinforcement of their names contributed to their self-esteem
and sense of identity.)

The therapist now introduced the autoharp as accompaniment for D and her mother to ventilate feelings through

metaphoric lyrics. The therapist shared the autoharp with D first. P spontaneously picked up the maracas. After they sang one verse of "Someone's singing, Kumbaya," the therapist asked, "Now, what else can someone do?" D answered, "crying." They all sang, "Someone's crying, Kumbaya." D sang very sadly, dramatizing how a person would feel if she were crying. (This metaphoric use of lyrics is effective in eliciting statements of many hidden feelings and proved to be a significant experience for D as she was able to reveal her own hidden feelings. The therapist and D could return to this point at another session and further explore her sadness.) At P's turn, she chose happy to sing about and said she was happy when "you don't have problems and everything is good." This, too, was a revealing message for D, who seemed to be unaware of her mother's feelings. D enthusiastically joined her mother's singing and both appeared truly happy singing and strumming together. (Through the metaphoric lyrics, they could reveal their hidden feelings in this first affective step involving mother and daughter.)

The therapist then introduced a standing maneuver to enable mother and child to interact in a rocking nurturing maneuver and continue the pleasure of the previous maneuver. Again, D took the initiative and began to show her mother how to hold the elastic rope and pull. Rather than instruct P, or silence D, the therapist moved onto P's side as a model and began chanting, "pull-ing, pull-ing, back and forth" while rocking with her. As P assumed the reciprocal motion with her daughter, the therapist stepped away and continued chanting to maintain the structure for P and D. They also joined the chanting to accompany their movement and maintained eye contact with each other. To continue their mutual satisfaction, the therapist improvised lyrics to give each a sense of her own identity. "Mommy pulls D, Mommy pulls D, she pulls slowly, she pulls slowly." Then "D pulls Mommy, she pulls slow." Then they pulled fast and both laughed with joy. D hugged her mother and her mother put her arms around her daughter. (D looked happy but surprised at this show of affection.) It was apparent that P cared for D but was unable to communicate her affection because of her own unmet needs and anxiety.)

Since both seemed to want to continue this type of movement interaction, the therapist introduced another standing maneuver. (An ongoing goal in Paraverbal Communication is to reinforce pleasure with a repeated similar yet different experience.) This copying maneuver reinforced another important interaction, that of D imitating her mother. After this, D could be appropriately nurtured as her mother validated her actions by copying her. The therapist structured the maneuver to first enable P to initiate a movement for D and the therapist to copy. The therapist sang, "Whatever Mommy does, we'll do like Mommy" and waited. P stood and gestured to communicate that she did not know what to do. As D stepped in to help her mother again, the therapist merely repeated the lyrics, and at the completion, P waved her arms in the air as her contribution. (The repetition of the lyrics stimulated P to participate.) Both D and the therapist imitated her and continued the chanting. Then at D's turn to lead and be imitated, as they chanted, "Whatever D does, we'll do like she does," D eagerly anticipated her part and made a sophisticated dance motion and spun around. Her mother smiled and watched as the therapist copied her. D spun around again to show her mother how she did it. The therapist again chanted, "Whatever D does, we'll do like she does" to accompany D's action and to provide structure for P, and then gestured for P to join her in the spinning movement. She turned around slowly with a smile on her face. D clapped her hands in approval of her mother's imitation. (Through this imitative strategy, it was so apparent that, while needing and requesting nurture for herself, D was providing nurture for her mother. A smile and look of contentment on P's face communicated this message.) The therapist continued to structure all the maneuvers to thus provide this mutual nurture for both D and P.

For the final maneuver, the therapist introduced chalking to music to enable both mother and daughter to create and then see their own unique visual products, stimulated by rhythmic sound, color, and freedom of movement. The therapist placed D and her mother on either side of an easel with many colors of chalk available in front of them. As the rhythmic march began, D moved her body in a swaying movement and made bold strokes. She often peeked around the easel to see what her mother was doing. P was making small circles and remained involved in her chalking design. D returned to her own chalking but checked back frequently to watch her mother. At the end of the march, both put down the chalk and looked at their products. D immediately ran to her mother's side and asked if she had liked the chalking. Her mother nodded. D praised her mother's work. Since P did not reciprocate and praise her daughter's work, the therapist pointed out the interesting strokes D had made and encouraged her mother to comment on her daughter's creation. (Through this maneuver and interaction with the therapist, P learned how to praise her daughter by observing and then modeling the therapist's behavior.)

This Paraverbal session provided many interactive experiences for both D and P and began to reverse the dysfunctional mother–child relationship. Through the interactive maneuvers, D began to experience mother's nurture through P's simple imitation but significant validation of her. P also experienced pleasure through the sensorimotor maneuvers and the resultant pleasure from the natural mother–child interaction. Through the therapist's comments about D's competence and P's own positive impact upon her daughter, she has begun to recognize D as an individual with her own strengths, but also her own needs. Because of P's own development, the therapist could now work to structure maneuvers to develop a stronger sense of identity for both mother and child. Many maneuvers such as chanting names and using the unique ideas of mother and child had been introduced in this session to reinforce personal identity. Each had opportunities to ventilate personal feelings and talk about them, thereby further illuminating mother and daughter's individual sense of identity.

Session 3

In the second session with her daughter, P was able at times to provide newly gained appropriate leadership for D through the structure of the maneuvers. A primary objective was to increase P's appropriate nurturing and modeling for D. (Their daily roles have been sharply reversed with the mother taking behavioral cues from D. D's facility with the English language was better than her mother's and as a result, D was called upon to interpret and often to handle matters.) In the Paraverbal session, P had opportunities to initiate pleasurable actions and thereby elicit positive, cooperative responses from D. She in turn showed her great pleasure in this more natural interaction with her mother.

For the first maneuver, D asked her mother which instrument she wished to use and then handed her the castanets. P accepted them and spontaneously clicked them together. D picked up a drum and imitated her mother's pattern. The therapist commented on their skillful rhythmic tapping. Then, to provide opportunity for P to initiate rather than have D instruct and choose for her, the therapist suggested that P might want to choose some other material. She smiled and asked to use the autoharp and to sing another song about good times and having fun. (P learned that her daughter and she were accepted and, because of P's improved self-esteem, she was able to make choices more easily.) The therapist placed the autoharp between P and herself. D now spontaneously picked up the castanets that her mother had used and clicked them together as the therapist began to chant, "I'm on my way, and I won't come back, I'm on my way, and I won't come back." P echoed her words following the therapist's invitation to do so. She then asked P to improvise more words and decide where they could go in the song. P responded, "To the beach—swimming." The therapist praised her for her contribution and sang the lyrics. D and her mother joined, "We'll go to the beach and we'll go swimming." P, feeling the safety of the lyrics, then offered that she and D would go swimming. D nodded eagerly. The therapist incorporated these significant words into the song and they all sang, "D and Mommy will go to the beach, and they'll go swimming."

To continue their mutual pleasure and increase P's involvement with her daughter, the therapist introduced a song about D growing up. The therapist now placed the autoharp between P and D, so that they could face each other for the maneuver, and sang, "When D was a baby, a baby, a baby, she went this way and that way." To further develop P in her nurturing role, the therapist asked her to show them a movement that D made as a baby. P said she couldn't hold D because she weighed only two pounds and that D had to stay in the hospital for three months. (This was pertinent historical information which illuminated the situation for D. The song maneuver evoked long lost experiences and provided D with some meager vision of her past.) D then spontaneously responded and dramatized how she cried when she was a baby. The therapist reinforced the experience and made it current by incorporating D's crying into the song. To elicit some description of her daughter's later years, the therapist then sang, "When D was four, she went this way and that way," and looked to P to complete the phrase. She responded, "She talked little words and played." D looked nurtured and pleased at the thought of herself growing and her mother's recognition of her actions. The therapist then incorporated the new lyrics and all sang, "When D was four, she talked little words and played." The therapist then let them know that she would sing a new verse and told them to listen and think about the words they wanted to improvise.

She sang, "When D was eight, she went this way and that way." D looked at her mother and spontaneously sang, "She talks" and her mother supportively added, "And she dances." D appeared joyously showered with so many happy images and laughingly added, "and plays and takes a bath." (The happy images evoked by the improvised song lyrics further contributed to D's raised self-image and sense of identity.) The therapist incorporated all of D and P's words into the song and they all sang.

To provide opportunities for both mother and daughter to have choices and reinforce their respective senses of identity, the therapist introduced a variety of drums and offered P first choice. She chose a drum with furry sides. D chose the large floor drum. The therapist suggested that P begin by tapping a pattern. She tapped a rapid one and the therapist and D imitated her. P nodded in approval of the imitation, and then they all tapped the rapid pattern synchronously three times. To encourage P's leadership as mother, the therapist suggested she tap the pattern in different ways such as soft, loud, fast, and slow and that D and she would imitate her. P smiled at each step—her own tapping and then at the validation of it. Then the therapist suggested D tap a pattern for P and the therapist to copy. D eagerly prepared to tap, asked if they were ready, and then tapped the same pattern her mother had tapped. P smiled as she recognized her own pattern, and the therapist commented that D wanted to be like her mother. P leaned toward D to assist her and demonstrated on D's drum another original pattern. (The mother, for the first time, was assuming an appropriate role with her daughter.) D listened attentively and then said, "I'll do it" and tapped the same pattern her mother had shown her. (P, unaccustomed to D's cooperation, looked very pleased.) The therapist and P immediately imitated her. Then D rubbed the top of the drum with sweeping motions. The therapist commented that it looked like she was dusting and D responded, "I clean at home; if

there's a lot of things on the floor, I pick them up." The therapist then rhythmically imitated her motion and encouraged
P to do the same while chanting, "This is how D cleans at
home." D laughed and seemed to enjoy the acceptance of her
spontaneous ideas.

The therapist ended the tapping maneuver with individual name tapping, beginning with D. All joined in and
chanted the syllables of her name. Then the therapist demonstrated how each of them could chant a different syllable
of D's name at her turn. In this way, all could participate in
tapping each other's names. This was a good exercise in impulse control for both D and her mother. Each was motivated
to wait her turn by the promised pleasure of hearing her
own name and the pleasurable reciprocal interaction. They
repeated the maneuver with P, and then the therapist's
name. For an additional impulse control experience, she
demonstrated how P could tap and chant D's first name and
then D could tap and chant her last name. They asked to do
the same with D's name.

For the final maneuver, the therapist introduced the
chalking maneuver that would enable both to stand and experience the pleasure of freedom of movement (after a long
seated maneuver) while chalking to the stimulation of
rhythmic sound. They had both enjoyed this maneuver in
the last session. D got up eagerly and prepared to chalk. D
took her place and reflectively chose two bright colors. As
the rhythmic music began, both had their eyes closed and
moved their arms with the rhythm as they had done during
the last session. When the therapist said, "Go," they opened
their eyes and both began to chalk in their own unique manner. D chalked by filling in large vertical sections of the paper with solid color. Her mother made many rows of small
script-like letters across the paper. At the bottom, she wrote
D. D continued filling the paper and at the completion, drew
a frame around the paper. Both admired each other's works
and D was overjoyed at seeing her name on her mother's colorful work.

In this second session with her daughter, P showed personal growth, and development in the quality of the mother–daughter interaction was apparent. As P received nurture through the interactive maneuvers, her self-confidence as a mother grew. As her self-confidence grew, she was more able to nurture D. Thus, because of the structure inherent in the Paraverbal maneuvers, the mother–child interaction proceeded more appropriately. P took satisfaction in being consulted for her ideas and in the validation she received through imitation. Although she was unaccustomed to providing appropriate leadership for D, she began to enjoy and assume this role with the therapist's support. Because of her mother's more appropriate behavior and her own ventilation of feelings, D experienced less anxiety and seemed to more freely resume her role as an 8-year-old child. As a result, she was developing cognitively, learning new words and language facility, and expressing her thoughts clearly, which had been a problem in school. She enthusiastically participated in all maneuvers and remained actively involved, spontaneously making suggestions and initiating variations. She learned to wait her turn and was behaving in a less intrusive manner. This development was significant because of D's initial difficulty in relationships with classmates. Through the interactive maneuvers, she learned to more effectively reciprocate in a relationship. She has had opportunities to listen to expressions of feelings and then be listened to by another person. Through this process, she was beginning to empathize with others and behave accordingly. D's reported stubbornness and rebelliousness were not evident in the sessions. She did not feel the need to be resistant or oppositional as her needs for recognition were satisfied through reciprocal leadership opportunities in the maneuvers and also through the nurture she received. By having opportunities to take the lead at times and then to imitate at other times, she experienced the satisfaction of reciprocal leadership. She learned the pleasure of relatedness and sharing. D had many opportunities to demonstrate her mastery, experience pleasure, and feel accepted through the Paraverbal maneuvers. In this way, her oppositional behavior was replaced by positive participation.

Results

Paraverbal sessions continued with many more pleasurable interactive experiences for both D and her mother. While P could not attend the sessions regularly, the therapist continued to structure the maneuvers to enable D to receive nurture from the therapist. (For example, on D's birthday, the therapist improvised lyrics about her special day and past birthdays.) In a maneuver designed to appropriately regress D to receive missed nurture, the therapist introduced a body movement maneuver that permitted D to assume an infantile position and then unfold. The therapist chanted, "D is rolled up like a ball, like a ball, like a ball—now she is growing very tall, very tall, very tall," while D dramatized the lyrics. She was extremely happy rolled up and then gradually grew tall by standing on a chair and raising her arms in the air. Through many maneuvers involving dramatization, D improvised lyrics and movements, receiving further nurture through interaction with the therapist. During one such movement maneuver, D walked playfully on plastic walking cups and improvised lyrics about the different kinds of steps she was taking, "giant steps, baby steps." The therapist provided further nurture as she rhythmically accompanied her movements. D frequently requested a maneuver in which the therapist and she danced together and each improvised movements: "D, come and dance with me." In addition, D ventilated feelings through metaphoric lyrics. After singing with the therapist "Nobody Knows the Trouble I've Seen," D talked about her own troubles that resulted from breaking an object and being punished. (The metaphoric song stimulated her to reveal hidden fear and guilt that caused her much anguish. She frequently requested this song that she knew would provide emotional relief.) She was also able to ventilate her anger toward specific individuals by blowing and breaking soap bubbles. Another way she ventilated was by using large cymbals to first dramatize feelings such as happy, sad, scared, and mad. She gained further nurture by the intimacy of guessing the therapist's feelings from her dramatizations. These dramatizations provided a bridge to the next step—discussion of the feelings. Additional goals in the sessions were designed to develop D's auditory processing and memory through the sound maneuvers. They were a bridge to help her with her learning difficulties, which could now be addressed. Through the rhythmic structure of the tapping maneuvers, D was able to recall sequences of names of animals, body parts, and clothing, friends and favorite activities in school by rhythmically tapping these words as she articulated the words. The tactile stimulation and categories provided the context for her and she ably and pleasurably recalled the words for each category (cat–tiger–lion; elbow–knee–ankle–foot). She demonstrated the ability to learn in a situation in which context is provided. D further developed her language ability through the variety of the maneuvers as she dramatized actions and improvised lyrics. She chanted, "The best fun is to go to the park and play on the swings" as she and the therapist used the rope to rhythmically pull and rock back and forth. D improvised, "Now we swing up," "Now we jump together," "Now we shake our shoulders," and many more action statements while she and the therapist synchronously dramatized her ideas.

Through Paraverbal Communication, D has experienced the nurture that had been missing. She experienced it from the therapist but also, significantly, from her mother as they interacted synchronously and reciprocally through the use of sound and movement maneuvers. Both experienced pleasure. P through her own pleasurable interactions, has learned ways to begin to meet her daughter's needs for nurture and guidance. D's self-esteem has improved significantly and she has increasingly interacted appropriately with her mother and the therapist as the sessions progressed.

Summary

In the two illustrations of Paraverbal Communication used to develop mother–child interaction, all participants developed more appropriate behavior. The children experienced the needed nurture through acceptance and pleasurable interaction with their mothers. They developed new functional behavior to which their mothers could respond. Both mothers, for whom the therapist was a model, likewise experienced nurture through pleasurable interaction with their children and, as a result, became more aware of their own and their children's needs. The Paraverbal maneuvers provided flexible, pleasureful ways for the mothers and children to interact, both nonverbally and verbally. Movement was often the therapeutic interaction of choice, and, at other times, sound was needed for efficacy, according to the observed behavior of mother and child. Through pleasurable, reciprocal interactions and acceptance of the unique individual choices of both mothers and children, communication developed as did appropriate relationships. Paraverbal Communication has helped to establish appropriate relationships, through which these mothers and children can continue to develop in healthy, positive ways.

12

How Parents Can Use Paraverbal Communication Principles at Home with Their Children

The most significant way a parent can assist a child is by truly understanding what makes him want to engage in positive behavior. This understanding often requires a change of attitude on the part of the parent who often has had to deal with resistant and otherwise difficult behavior.

This chapter will suggest ways that parents can reinforce the new appropriate behavior that their children learn through Paraverbal Communication. One of the fundamental elements of Paraverbal Communication is the acceptance of the child by the professional (therapist) with whom the child is working. Parents, too, can meaningfully reinforce and demonstrate their own acceptance of their child as a significant way of assisting in their child's development. How this is done is illustrated further on in the chapter. A second basic element of Paraverbal Communication that greatly contributes to progress is that the child experiences pleasure through the therapeutic interactions with the therapist. As a result, the child is eager to repeat the experience and, thus, he participates in his own development. The parent can also significantly assist in this process.

Parents who begin to respond to their children in constructive ways that provide acceptance and pleasure will obtain increased positive responses in turn from them. Parents who reinforce what the child has experienced in the Paraverbal Communication sessions, will be helping their children toward optimal development.

Many children are referred for therapeutic assistance because of difficulties with learning; others, because of their inability to interact appropriately with others. Frequently, parents and children do not communicate effectively, and as a result, parents often have difficulty managing their children. The reasons are many and varied, but underlying most poor communication is often a misunderstanding of feelings and ideas.

Paraverbal Communication Principles

Before specific parental suggestions are offered it is important for parents to understand the purpose of Paraverbal Communication. Simply stated, the primary purpose of the intervention is to make it possible for children to communicate their feelings and ideas in ways that are simple and non-threatening. Through the Paraverbal Communication approach, children have many opportunities to discharge their feelings nonverbally using a variety of sensorimotor materials and percussion instruments. These materials make it easier for children to communicate their feelings than through words alone. After experiencing these safe and pleasurable nonverbal interactions, children frequently move toward verbal communication, often through metaphoric song lyrics whose messages parallel their own troubling situations. Through the use of lyrics found in folk and popular songs, discussion can more readily take place around someone else's similar situation (the person in the song). Therefore, children feel safe communicating their opinions and often take the next step quite spontaneously to relate the situation in the song lyrics to their own. Communication has progressed. Once children feel free to communicate their feelings, they become more trusting and more receptive to therapeutic intervention for the difficulties that have interfered with their development.

A major objective in every Paraverbal Communication session is to enhance the child's self-esteem. The child may rarely experience a sense of competence in daily tasks and interactions and as a result lack self-confidence. These situations diminish the child's self-esteem and often leave him frustrated, angry, and vulnerable to anxiety and conflict with others and himself.

To alleviate the frustration and enable the child to feel good about himself, impromptu learning and social situations are spontaneously introduced in the Paraverbal sessions. This is done to ensure that the child experiences mastery. All therapeutic interactions take place with a therapist who accepts the child no matter what level of functioning. The Paraverbal materials appeal to and are appropriate for children of all ages, and the activities or maneuvers are introduced specifically for each child's needs. Because each child is free to make choices of materials and movements, he quickly learns that it can be good to take the initiative, suggest ideas, and decide how he wishes to communicate. The child feels that he is accepted. Additional positive interactions result from planned repetition in the Paraverbal sessions, which enables the child to experience mastery because of the predictability of the repeated experiences. Because the materials and ways of using them are varied, the child's interest is maintained. As a result of the child's success and pleasure in the maneuvers, he is generally eager to repeat the pleasurable experiences and even take the initiative through additional Paraverbal maneuvers. This willingness and new ability to interact with the therapist is the first step toward trust and makes it possible for the child to make progress.

Just what is it that causes the child's self-esteem to improve by engaging in the Paraverbal maneuvers? First of all, the child is intrigued by the attractive sensorimotor materials and is eager to use them. He has many opportunities to demonstrate and experience his uniqueness through the novel ways they can be used. Since the materials are simple to use and can be used in many imaginative ways, the child can use them in his own unique manner. Therefore, he need not fear failure. Another factor that contributes to the child's self-esteem is the positive and pleasurable feelings he receives for interaction with the therapist. There are opportunities for simultaneously interacting along with the therapist as well as ones in which the child responds spontaneously, as the situation suggests, in a reciprocal exchange. Through these interactions, in which the child experiences the positive and reinforcing effects of mutual interaction, he feels that he is worthwhile and accepted.

Parental Involvement

Although it is the teachers and mental health professionals who apply the specific Paraverbal Communication principles and techniques to children, it is the parents who can reinforce their new behavior in their daily interactions with them by applying the same principles. By understanding the Paraverbal objectives for their children and reasons that the therapist uses specific activities or "maneuvers" in Paraverbal Communication, parents can begin to respond to their children in new constructive ways consistent with those used in their child's Paraverbal Communication sessions.

When parents are with their child, they can demonstrate acceptance by communicating an understanding of what the child is feeling and letting him know they support him. For example, a parent can learn to accept the 10-year-old child's angry outburst, knowing that by simply ventilating his anger, the child is, in a typical manner, beginning to address the problem. If the parent is aware that preadolescent children feel vulnerable and have fears and worries about growing up, he can be more accepting of the resultant behavior that is so often resistant and difficult. Knowing that children at this age are engaged in an active search for self and on this account often reject those persons closest to them is helpful in itself to the parent. As the child is highly critical of himself at this stage of development, he only feels more alienated when parents also find fault with him. The preadolescent is hungry for praise and will put it to good developmental use if it is offered appropriately and genuinely. Simple comments from a parent such as, "Thank you for helping your younger brother with his bike," "You really know how to fix things," or "You look great in that color," contribute to the child's self-esteem and demonstrate to the child a parent's acceptance of him.

A frequent referral problem is the child who resists the parent's attempts at helping him to grow up. The child does not do what the parent wishes, and, as a result, there is conflict between them. By understanding what the child really wants and needs, a parent can begin to provide for their child's needs as well as improve their interaction. For example, regardless of the situation that may cause resistance, a parent can offer the resistant child a choice. Instead of resisting, a child can actually take pleasure in making his own choice of such things as toys, food, times to go to bed, activities before bedtime, places to visit, or whatever the circumstances. By offering a choice, "Would you like to have me read to you or should we play a game before bedtime?" or "Should we take tiny steps or giant steps upstairs?" a child feels the needed sense of validation and control and need not become oppositional to assert himself.

There are many opportunities for parents to apply Para-verbal Communication principles with young children to better understand them. For example, when a parent senses that a child feels angry or sad, he can encourage the child to "dramatize" what he is feeling by showing this feeling on his face or through the use of his body. The parent can then further encourage the child by telling him what she thinks he's feeling and showing her. If a child is hesitant in showing what he is feeling, the parent can playfully model for the child, the communication of a feeling, perhaps dramatizing anger by making punching motions in the air and showing an angry face. The parent can then ask the child to guess her feeling. Other emotions such as sad, scared, and happy can also be dramatized and communicated in the same way. Once the feelings are out in the open, parent and child then have an opportunity to talk about these previously hidden emotions. In this pleasurable way, the parent is providing the child with an opportunity to make progress in his development and communicate.

Parents can further develop the parent–child relationship by participating in activities that the child favors and has mastered. This type of pleasurable interaction with a familiar and already mastered activity pleases the child because he experiences a sense of his own competence. During the interaction, he also experiences the parent's pride in him and significantly, the parent's acceptance of him. For example, after the child has mastered a simple activity, such as tossing a ball into the air and catching it, a parent can encourage further development by suggesting variations of that activity for the child. The parent can say, "Now let's toss it up and catch it two times," "Now you toss the ball to me and I'll toss it back to you," or "This time you tell me how to toss the ball." Through these simple interactions, the child is pleasurably challenged and further develops in significant ways, because he is gaining new abilities and experiencing new pleasure with the parent.

There are many ways to strengthen the parent–child relationship once this kind of pleasurable interaction has begun. By chanting words in a song-like manner to describe a child's movement, a parent can provide him with structure for purposeful activity as well as reinforce their pleasurable relationship. For example, a parent can chant, "Jimmy tosses the ball to Mommy," or "Now we take a giant step, now a tiny step, now what kind of step should we take?" as the mother accompanies the child up the stairs to bed. This type of chanting of descriptive words and phrases provides structure for the child and pleasurably encourages appropriate behavior and well-being between parent and child.

Imitation is still another technique used in Paraverbal Communication sessions that helps the child's development and can be easily incorporated by the parent in daily interactions. Since imitation is the essential way that young children learn, this natural technique is effective in creating a closer relationship between parents and children. Imitation can be done in a gamelike manner with the parent imitating the child and then child imitating the parent. Simple tasks around the house such as putting toys away, getting ready for bed, or getting dressed for school can provide such situations. Clapping of hands, stamping of feet, and other such movements are actions that children enjoy imitating as well as creating. When a parent imitates a child's action, he is validating what it is that the child does. Once again, the child feels accepted.

As is apparent, many opportunities exist for shared pleasure in daily play situations between parent and child. Blowing soap bubbles is an example. A parent can blow the bubbles and tell the child to break them, either by clapping them in his hands or stamping on them, or he can be encouraged to break them in his own way. A comment of praise is appropriate after the child breaks the bubbles: "I like the ways you stamped on the bubbles" or "I never thought of breaking them with my knee. What a good idea." This praise applies to an action in which the child himself has just participated and, therefore, the parent's recognition of his mastery is very meaningful to him.

Storytelling provides another ideal opportunity for shared parent–child interaction. A parent might begin a story and ask the child to create simple sound effects when appropriate. For example, in the story *The Little Engine That Could*, a child can be asked to make the sound of the engine trying to climb the hill: "Was it a loud sound or a soft sound?" "Was it fast or slow?" Children are empowered and involved when made part of the story in this way. By thus involving the child so pleasurably with the parent, the relationship becomes even stronger. Any story can be utilized in this way and stories already known to children can be retold and revitalized in this new interactive way.

These techniques are just a few of the many possibilities offered to parents to utilize when applying the Paraverbal principles of acceptance and pleasure in their interactions with their children. Paraverbal Communication is unique in its ability to help children ventilate feelings safely and thereby communicate them. In Paraverbal Communication sessions, children learn new appropriate behavior because they do feel free to communicate. The freedom and ability to communicate feelings and thoughts is necessary for cognitive or behavioral development to take place. When the child's newly learned appropriate behavior is reinforced outside the Paraverbal Communication sessions, children experience in new and significant settings the benefits and relevance of their behavioral change. Parents can greatly assist their children in this important development. They can provide an environment in which their children feel free to use their newly learned interactive skills, receive reinforcement from their parents for their behavioral gains, and therefore master the ability to communicate.

References

Chapter 2

Frank, L. 1971. Tactile communication. In *The rhetoric of nonverbal communication.* H. Basmajian, ed. Glenview, IL: Scott, Foresman.

Heimlich, Evelyn P. 1973. Using a patient as "assistant therapist" in Paraverbal Therapy. *Int J Child Psychother* 2:13–52.

Mittleman, B. 1954. Motility in infants, children, and adults. *Psychoanal Study Child* 9:142–177.

Chapter 4

Belmont, I., Belmont, L., and Birch, H. G. 1969. The perceptual organization of complex arrays by educable mentally subnormal children. *J Nerv Ment Dis* 149: 241–252.

Berko, M. J. 1969. *Communication training in childhood brain damage.* Springfield, IL: Thomas.

Birch, H. G., ed. 1964. *Brain damage in children.* Baltimore: Williams and Wilkins, p. 69.

Boll, T. J., and Reitan, R. M. 1972. Motor and tactile perceptual deficits in brain damaged children. *Percept Mot Skills* 34:343–350.

Canino, Ian A., Earley, Brian F., and Rogler, Lloyd H. 1980. *The Puerto Rican child in New York City: Stress and mental health.* New York: Hispanic Research Center, Fordham University, p. 50.

Chalfont, James C., and Scheffelin, Margaret A. 1969. *Central processing dysfunctions in children. A review of research.* Bethesda, MD: U.S. Dept. of Health, Education, and Welfare, pp. 13, 15, 19.

Christensen, A. L. 1975. *Luria's neuropsychological investigation.* New York: Spectrum.

Eaves, L. C., Kendall, D. C., and Crichton, M. B. 1972. The early detection of minimal brain dysfunction. *J Learning Disabil* 5:5.

Gardner, Richard A. 1979. *The objective diagnosis of minimum brain dysfunction.* Cresskill, NJ: Creative Therapeutics, p. XV, 151.

Gartner, Alan, and Lipsky, Dorothy Kerzner. 1987. Beyond special education: Toward a quality system for all students. *Harv Educ Rev* 57:371–372.

Gustavson, J. L., Golden, C. J. *et al.* 1982. The Luria-Nebraska Neurophysiological Battery—Children's Revision: Current research findings. Paper presented at the meeting of the American Psychological Association, Washington DC.

Halstead, W. C. 1947. *Brain and intelligence.* Chicago: University of Chicago Press.

Heimlich, E. P. 1972. Paraverbal techniques in the therapy of childhood disorders. *Int J Child Psychother* 1:65–83.

Heimlich, E. P. 1975. An auditory-motor percussion test for differential diagnosis of children with communication difficulties. *Percep Mot Skills* 40:839–845.

Jansky, Jeannette, and de Hirsch, Katrina 1972. *Preventing reading failure. Prediction, diagnosis, intervention.* New York: Harper and Row, pp. 8, 16.

Luria, A. 1966. *Higher cortical functions in man.* New York: Basic Books.

Minski, L. 1957. *Deafness, mutism and mental deficiency in children.* London: Heinemann.

Myklebust, H. R. 1954. *Auditory disorders in children.* New York: Grune and Stratton.

Reitan, R. M. 1970. Sensory motor functions, intelligence and cognition and emotional status in subjects with cerebral lesions. *Percept Mot Skills* 31:275–284.

Reitan, R. M., and Boll, T. J. 1971. Intellectual and cognitive functions in Parkinson's disease. *J Consult Clin Psychol* 37:364–369.

Reitan, R. M., and Fitzburgh, K. B. 1971. Behavioral deficits in groups with cerebral vascular lesions. *J Consult Clin Psychol* 37:215–223.

Reitan, R. M., Reed, J. C., and Dyken, M. L. 1971. Cognitive psychomotor and motor correlates of multiple sclerosis. *J Nerv Ment Dis* 153:218–224.

Rudnick, M., Sterritt, G. M., and Flax, M. 1967. Auditory and visual rhythm perception and reading ability. *Child Dev* 38:581.

Smith, W. L. 1969. *Neuropsychological testing in organic brain dysfunction.* Springfield, IL: Thomas.

Stambach, M. 1951. Le probleme du rhythme dans le developpement de l'enfant et dans les dyslexies d'evolution. *Enfance* 4:480–502.

Stevens, D. A., Boydstun, J. A., Dykman, R. A., Peters, J. E., and Sinton, D. W. 1967. Presumed minimal brain dysfunction in children. *Arch Gen Psychiatry* 16:281–285.

Chapter 6

Fields, B. 1954. Music as an adjunct in the treatment of brain-damaged children. *Am J Phys Med* 33:273–283.

Garden, H. 1973. *The quest for mind: Piaget, Levi-Strauss, and the structuralist movement.* New York: Alfred A. Knopf.

Gartner, Alan, and Lipsky, Dorothy K. 1987. Beyond special education: Toward a quality system for all students. *Harv Educ Rev* 57:367–395.

Gerhardt, L. A. 1973. *Moving and knowing.* Englewood Cliffs, NJ: Prentice-Hall.

Ginnot, H. G. 1961. *Group psychotherapy with children.* New York: McGraw-Hill.

Ginsburg, H., and Opper, S. 1969. *Piaget's theory of intellectual development: An introduction.* Englewood Cliffs, NJ: Prentice-Hall.

Heimlich, E. 1972. Paraverbal techniques in the therapy of childhood communication disorders. *Int J Child Psychother* 1:79.

Wiig, E. H., and Semel, E. M. 1976. *Language disabilities in children and adolescents.* Columbus, OH: Charles E. Merrill.

Chapter 8

Bender, L. 1952. Personal communication.

Creak, E. M. 1963. Childhood psychosis. *Brit J Psychiatry* 109:84–89.

Escalona, S., and Bergman, P. 1949. Unusual sensitivities in very young children. In *Psychoanalytic study of the child.* New York: International Universities Press, pp. 3–4.

Frank, L. 1971. Tactile communication. In *The rhetoric of nonverbal communication.* H. Bosmajian, ed. Glenview, IL: Scott, Foresman.

Freud, Anna. 1946. *The psychoanalytic treatment of children.* London: Imago.

Heimlich, E. P. 1972. Paraverbal techniques in the therapy of childhood disorders. *Int J Child Psychother* 1:65–83.

Howlin, Patricia, & Rutter, M. 1987. *Treatment of autistic children.* New York: Wiley.

Kanner, L. 1958. The specificity of early infantile autism: The concept of infantile autism. *Rev Psychiatric Infant* 25:113.

Kanner, L., and Eisenberg, L. 1955. The specificity of early infantile autism: Notes on the follow-up studies of autistic children. In *Psychopathology of childhood.* P. Hoch and J. Rubin, eds. New York: Grune and Stratton.

Mahler, M. 1975. *Psychological birth of the human infant. Symbiosis and individuation.* New York: Basic Books.

Mahler, M. 1952. On child psychosis and schizophrenia: Autistic and symbiotic infantile psychosis. *Psychoanal Study Child* 7:286–305.

Simon, Baron-Cohen. 1988. Better communicative skills. *J Autism Dev Disorders* 18(3):379–397.

Stern, D. 1985. *The interpersonal world of the infant.* New York: Basic Books.

Chapter 9

Coles, R. R. 1971. Top songs in the sixties: A content analysis of popular lyrics. *Am Behav Sci* 14:398.

Coles, R. R. 1986. *The political life of children.* New York: The Atlantic Monthly Press.

Erikson, E. 1963. *Childhood and society.* New York: Norton, p. 262.

Fischer, C., and Herkes, D. 1985. What entertainers are doing to your kids. *U.S. News and World Rep* 99:46.

Gardner, G. F. 1971. Aggression and violence—the enemies of precision learning in children. *Am J Psychiatry* 128:448.

Heimlich, E. 1983. The metaphoric use of song lyrics as paraverbal communication. *Child Psychiatry Hum Dev* 14:2.

Hirsch, P. 1971. Sociological approaches to the pop music phenomenon. *Am Behav Sci* 14:384.

Mark, Arlene. 1986. Adolescents discuss themselves and drugs through music. *J Substance Abuse Treat* 3:243–249.

Redl, F. 1966. *When we deal with children.* New York: The Free Press, p. 126.

Saari, C. 1986. The metaphor in therapeutic communication with young adolescents. *Child Adolescent Soc Work* 3(1):16–17.

Chapter 11

Ainsworth, M. D. S. 1977. Social development in the first year of life: Maternal influences on infant–mother attachment. In *Developments in psychiatric research: Essays based on the Sir Geoffrey Vickers lectures of the mental health foundation.* J. M. Tanner, ed. London: Hodder and Stoughton.

Alpert, Augusta. 1957. A special therapeutic technique for certain developmental disorders in prelatency children. *Am J Orthopsychiatry* 27:256.

Cohen, S. 1976. *Social and personality development in childhood.* New York: Macmillan, p. 97.

Erikson, Erik H. 1980. *Identity and the life circle.* New York: Norton, p. 58.

Mahler, Margaret S. 1972. Rapprochement subphase of the separation–individuation process. *Psychoanal Quar* 41(4):492.

Stern, Daniel N. 1974. The goal and structure of mother–infant play. *Am Acad Child Psychiatry.* 13:416.

About the Authors

EVELYN PHILLIPS HEIMLICH, former chairperson of Paraverbal Therapy and research associate at the New York State Psychiatric Institute, was also assistant adjunct professor of Paraverbal Therapy at the College of New Rochelle. At present she is consultant at St. Luke's–Roosevelt Hospital Child Psychiatry Department, as well as consultant at Barnard School New Rochelle Board of Education.

At New York State Psychiatric Institute Child Psychiatry Department, she treated inaccessible children who did not respond to traditional approaches. During this same period, she gave seminars in the Paraverbal method to resident child psychiatrists, nurses, and others in related fields.

Ms. Heimlich has lectured on Paraverbal Therapy at the University of Colorado Medical Center Child Psychiatry Department, the Hampstead Clinic in London, the

Queretaro Hospital in Queretaro, Mexico, and many other institutions.

ARLENE MARK received a Master of Arts in Special Education from Manhattanville College and a second Master's in School Psychology from the College of New Rochelle. She interned in Paraverbal Communication at the New York State Psychiatric Institute.

Most recently, Ms. Mark practiced Paraverbal Communication as School Psychologist at Lincoln Hall Residential Treatment Center for inner-city juvenile offenders in Lincolndale, New York. She developed adolescent communication skills through metaphoric use of popular song lyrics. She also treated children using Paraverbal Communication in private practice, and has written numerous articles for lay and professional periodicals in her field.

Ms. Mark works with New York City Special Education adolescents as class sponsor and Executive Committee Member of the "I Have a Dream" program. She is co-chairman of the New York Mentoring Advisory Committee and Professional Advisory Board Member of the National Center for Learning Disabilities.

Index